Jolly Super

by the same author

HOW TO STAY MARRIED
HOW TO SURVIVE FROM NINE TO FIVE

Jolly Super

JILLY COOPER

Methuen & Co Ltd

First published in 1971
by Methuen & Co Ltd
11 New Fetter Lane, London EC4
Copyright © Jilly Cooper, 1969, 1970, 1971

Printed in Great Britain
by Butler & Tanner Ltd
Frome and London

SBN 416 67220 5

To my parents

My thanks are due to the editors of *Harper's Bazaar* and *The Sunday Times*, in which these articles first appeared.

Contents

1 Women Friends

One of the most poignant stories I ever heard was of a small girl being taken out from school for the first time.

'Some girls walk in threes,' she said, 'and some girls walk in twos.'

'And what do you walk in?' asked her mother fondly.

'Oh, I walk in ones,' came the reply.

From the first moment I was cast into that snake pit – the kindergarten – I realized the necessity of getting on with my own sex and establishing a clique of best friends to giggle with and protect me from other little girls. Later when I went to boarding school, I was so terrified of walking in ones I always said 'yes' to whoever asked me to walk to church with them, which resulted in ghastly instances of quadruple dating.

It was at boarding school, too, that I learnt another golden rule: no friendship between women is so strong that a man cannot come between them. We used to have dances with the neighbouring boys' schools, and my year in the sixth we danced against Marlborough, who only provided sixty boys to eighty of us girls, I managed to angle every dance with the marvellous Captain of Squash, before he was lured away to the gooseberry bushes by my best friend, who was much prettier than I, and I was left to stumble heartbroken through the last waltz in the muscular arms of the biology mistress.

In fact I hated school so much that ever since then I've had a horror of occasions when more than four women are gathered together without men. I won't go to coffee mornings, or girls' lunches, or hen parties, I've stubbornly resisted learning bridge or getting involved in politics or good works. The

Rugger Wife Clique used to give me the shivers when I was first married, and at parties I always run a mile from groups of women talking about nappies and the price of fish.

But you've got to watch it – a woman is considered definitely suspect if she hasn't got any women friends:

'Man mad, nymphomaniac! Must be something wrong with her,' they whisper over the mail-order catalogue. Meaning she'll pay for it later when her looks go, and she can't get any men.

After I left school, I shared a warren in Tite Street with three other girls – one of them, who was not famed for the strength of her knicker elastic, had perfected a smoulderingly come-hither glance that could bring a man across a room in ten seconds flat.

My other flatmates and I, who were in far more often than she, used to spend hours practising our party smoulders on a large tin of Maxwell House:

'Now narrow your eyes, flare your nostrils, breathe deeply and think depraved, really depraved. I think she's got it, by George, she's got it.'

But living in each other's pockets, as we did, we were all deeply critical of each other's men, and it reached a stage when it was more important if your man pleased the rest of the flat than if he pleased you. Whenever I came proudly home with a new conquest, they would all gather round and take stock, emerging dripping from the bath, or out of bed in rollers – so insatiable was their curiosity.

If they rated him, everything was all right and he became a flat pet, if not they would disappear into the kitchen together and mutter over cups of coffe like the witches in *Macbeth*. Later, when he'd gone there would be a post mortem.

'Isn't he wildly attractive?' I would say defiantly.

'Yes, in a way, but if you think so, that's the important thing.'

'Nice little man,' another would chip in. 'Pity he sweats so much, and when did you start going for men with built-up shoes? I hope he doesn't go on like that about his mother when he's alone with you.'

And another romance would bite the dust.

10

Of course, once I got married, it all changed. If you have a really close relationship with a man, you don't need women friends so much. My husband makes me laugh far more than any woman. If something stunning happens I share it with him, if a crisis blows up I'm on the telephone to him in a flash, whereas before I was married I'd have run screaming to the nearest girlfriend.

And my husband doesn't encourage me to get too friendly with other women, he makes short work of any of my friends he doesn't like or considers unstable influences, and nothing irritates him more than hearing me and a chum indulging in women's talk:

'So you honestly think I can wear it without a bra/that stuff clogs the pores horribly/she's left him and gone off with the dentist and the furniture et cetera et cetera.'

As my father once said to my mother:

'I've nothing against other women, darling, except they make you so boring.'

But even if I can't stand women collectively, I do like and need them as individuals. Lunch with an attractive man always has the edge on lunch with an entertaining woman, but I'd far rather have lunch with an entertaining woman than a sexy but boring man. I relax and become mentally uncorseted with a girl as I never do with a man.

I remember being green with envy because a girlfriend was invited to trek up the Amazon with four really dolly men. She returned a nervous wreck, they'd all treated her like one of the boys.

'The thing I missed more than anything else,' she said, 'was a woman to giggle with and bitch about the men.'

I find generally that women need to talk about the opposite sex far more than men do. If a woman hooks a new man, she is compelled to rush out and tell a girlfriend. You see them nose to nose in coffee bars, at lunchtime, fat girls eating salads, thin girls eating spaghetti, drawing crosses in the brown sugar as they dissect last night's antics:

'He hasn't laid a finger on me yet.'

'Oh he can't be queer, he's married. Anyway he's asked me out again tomorrow, so let's have lunch the day after and I can tell you all about it.'

11

As I love *histoires,* I'm always very happy to down tools for half an hour and assume the role of friend as dustbin when a mate rings up with the latest saga of her love life. The narrative tension becomes almost unbearable, like a serial on television, one can hardly wait for the next instalment.

One misconception about friendship is that there's something wrong with you if you can't sustain a relationship over many years. 'Some of my best friends,' women claim smugly, 'are girls who were at school with me.'

They never bear in mind that people change and develop, and just because you shared a crush on Guy Mitchell with someone in '48, it doesn't mean you'll have anything in common with them today.

It's the same with office relationships. You can get incredibly close to girls you work with, laying booby traps for the office crone, speculating about the men in the office, and when you leave that particular job you vow to have lunch together every week. But as weeks go by, you find you have less and less in common, the atrocities of the ex-crone no longer seem of interest, and once a week becomes once a month – like a transistor battery running down, a spurt of conversation followed by longer and longer silences, until the relationship peters out altogether.

In the same way I often become friendly for short periods with people I've met on holiday, and in the past I've often struck up a friendship with a woman because she knew a man I was mad about, and I thought it would be a good way of getting through to him. Then the fancy would pass by, and the friendship would die. Equally I have girlfriends who only ring up when they're in trouble, or short of men; if I don't hear from them I know they're all right.

But how rarely, too, friends get on with friends.

'Do introduce me to Samantha,' cries Arabella. 'You've talked about her so much, I feel I already know her.'

When they do meet it's disastrous, instant hackles. They're both so used to your undivided attention they bitterly resent having to share it with someone else, and the moment you get home afterwards, they're both jamming the wires telling you how awful the other is.

Probably because women are in direct competition with one another, there's invariably a love-hate element in their relationship.

As La Rochefoucauld said: 'In the misfortunes of our best friends, we find something which is not displeasing to us.'

To be echoed three centuries later by Violet Elizabeth Bott: 'She's my best friend, I hate her.'

I cannot deny that I feel a stronger stab of jealousy if one of my best friends hooks a rich and gorgeous man, or her child gets a scholarship to Winchester, than if it happens to a mere acquaintance or even an enemy.

In the same way, never take your best friend's advice when buying clothes, as her motives won't be purely disinterested. And it's always your best friends who say you don't look a bit fat, and load potatoes on to your plate, when you're valiantly trying to diet.

And how beastly women are to each other. I know two girls, Caroline who is ravishing and twenty-six, and Jane who is beautiful and thirty-seven, and Jane is so jealous of Caroline that she makes a point of seducing all her men to prove she's more attractive. Actually it doesn't prove any such thing – merely that men never look a gift whore in the mouth.

Jane and Caroline were at a party recently where several of Caroline's exes were present and Jane chose a long silence to say: 'Hands up anyone who hasn't slept with Caroline.'

Yet they are the greatest of friends, ringing each other every day, getting endless stimulus from rowing, then making it up.

People always say how dreadful it is to be a fairweather friend, but I'd far rather have them than foulweather friends, who only love you when you're down, and immediately prick your bubbles when nice things happen to you.

I remember I was all starry-eyed with love when I was first married and a rich and unmarried girlfriend came to see me. She looked round our sparsely furnished flat and said: 'I suppose all your furniture's still in store.'

And some foulweather friends make a point of eroding your self-confidence: 'Samantha does get lumbered with some lame ducks.'

'Nonsense, she takes a perfectly healthy duck, breaks both its legs and sends it out into the world.'

But how do you drop people if you really don't like them and they cling on to you? At present my paranoia has reached an all-time high. A woman I know slightly (if you don't see her for six months, she's still exactly the same: perfectly bloody) has just rung up and said in a shrill voice: 'I haven't seen you for ages, everyone says you're so grand now, you're dropping all your old friends.'

Here was the golden opportunity but I, being wet, immediately said of course I wasn't dropping her, and why didn't she come round for a drink this evening, which means a row with my husband, who dislikes her even more than I do. The trouble is I long to be loved by everyone and therefore I run with the hare, the hounds, the fox, the horses, the huntsmen, the jolly farmers, not to mention the veiled ladies riding sidesaddle.

In the end I shall turn out as Oscar Wilde described Bernard Shaw: 'He hasn't an enemy in the world, and none of his friends like him.'

2 The Wages of Gin

Why do I love drink? I suppose because it takes the brakes off my inhibitions and kills my shyness. I like the feeling of irresponsibility as the worries roll off my back like Christian's burden at the wicket gate, and those lost misty afternoons after lunchtime sessions when I zigzag down the King's Road buying dresses I can't afford, ringing people I shouldn't, and generally making a nuisance of myself. Or those occasional evening parties when I seem to have shipped enough to float the QE2, and career round like a riderless horse in a steeplechase, thoroughly enjoying myself, potentially dangerous and quite out of control.

Not that I knock back all that much. Often I go for weeks without a drink, and I have only passed out once in my life when I got tight on Pimms at the age of eighteen. I had hated the taste of drink before that – but this concoction was not unpleasant. I had fourteen, keeled over, and had to be carried home like a coffin by four undergraduates.

I regained consciousness as they reached my digs in Polstead Road, shouting riotously for my landlady: 'Where, oh where, is the mistress of Bedstead Road?'

She was not amused, and even less so when she later found the most drunken of the undergraduates – now one of London's leading literary agents – stretched out on her sofa reading her laundry book. Shrilly, she asked him what he was doing.

'I'm very fond of reading laundry books,' he said gently. 'And I haven't read this one before, it's frightfully good.'

I had to leave at the end of the week.

Of course drinking isn't all jollity. There are those respectable dinner parties when you arrive from someone else's party and try to pretend you are sober – but your elbow keeps jerking off the edge of the table, you help yourself to salt three times, talk far too much, and finally betray yourself totally by trying to ring for a taxi on the answerphone.

Then there is the morning after, particularly after parties at home, when I totter downstairs with pounding skull and a tongue like rancid moss to be faced by chocolate mousse covered in cat's tongue marks and the Brie which has run off the cheese board on to the table.

Even worse are those times when you go to bed so late you are still tight when you wake up and you think you have escaped a hangover. Nemesis descends in a leisurely form about 10.30, when you are suddenly overcome with nausea in the fish queue or in the middle of a meeting.

The morning after is invariably followed by the mourning after. Those frantic telephone calls to ascertain how badly you have behaved. I always admire the cool of people who pretend to suffer from selective amnesia. One girl brought a friend's dinner party to a standstill recently by taking off her clothes during the pudding course. When she rang me next day, all she said was: 'Enjoy the cabaret, love?'

When people really can't remember what they did you can have great fun: 'You don't remember a thing? Well, the Thatchers will never ask you again . . . yes I'm afraid so – *all* over the Aubusson, and you can't go back to Overton's either, you took a slug at one of the waiters.'

Some Victorian spoke of the 'wild, rapturous, ineffable pleasure of drinking at someone else's expense', but it isn't all roses. There are those death-knell remarks: 'You must try some of Gideon's home-made beer', or 'Personally I can't tell this from Champagne'. Or the houses where they say come and have a drink, and mean it literally, and you sit chewing the lemon peel, and desperately drinking water from the ice as it melts.

Or those atrocious Glühwein parties, when people come home from ski-ing and try to re-create the atmosphere of the chalet: the hostess rushing round scarlet in the face, brandishing a saucepan of boiling Spanish Burgundy with half the kitchen cupboard thrown in.

The intelligent guests throw such drinks into the nearest potted plant, and search the oven and the lavatory cistern for the hard stuff. My husband once tipped a particularly nasty gin and something into the hostess's tropical fish tank. An hour later several white-bellied corpses floated to the surface, the wages of gin, I suppose.

Occasionally I make feeble attempts to go on the wagon – but it's travelling too fast. All my friends go off me, and attending parties is like watching a farce in a language I don't understand. It's even worse when someone you love gives up. January and February were hell last year when my husband stopped drinking. He became horribly puritanical, sourly sipping tomato juice and telling me I was going to the dogs every time I poured myself a second glass of sherry.

It always amuses me the excuses people give for drunkenness, 'His wife's just had a baby', or 'He hasn't been eating because he's on a diet'. Once my best friend brought her latest man to one of my parents' cocktail parties. After a while he disappeared into the loo, refusing to come out: 'Tim's terribly, terribly tired,' I kept hearing my girlfriend repeat to my mother as she tried to cover up the sounds of retching.

But the most endearing excuse I ever heard came from a man who said: 'I'm going to get absolutely plastered tonight, darling. I love you so much, I want to see two of you.'

3 Men's Liberation

Man the enemy and the oppressor: woman – the exploited and oppressed. Women's Lib have been hitting the headlines recently, grumbling about their lot, chucking bombs at Bob Hope and making concerted efforts to topple the patriarchal system. While sympathizing with many of the aims of Women's Lib, however, I think it is high time the men had their say.

Henpecked of the world unite, therefore, and raise the banner for Men's Lib. Your first objective must be to free men from the fear of being thought cissy. Why shouldn't a man have a good cry if he feels like it, why should he go to war, or be the one to crawl downstairs in search of burglars when the cat knocks over a milk bottle in the night?

If Women's Lib want a crack at the positions of power, they must forfeit their position of weakness. It will be men and children in future who will be helped solicitously into the first lifeboats, and the man who sits like a stuck pig in the car while his wife leaps out in the pouring rain, opens the door for him, and spikes her eyes out as she covers him with an umbrella.

Let us liberate men from the onus of being good in a crisis, from carrying heavy suitcases and opening doors for women, from having to make the agonizing decision of which wine to drink, and saying 'I say' to the waiter in a convincing voice when a caterpillar turns up in their wife's salad.

If women want free access to men's jobs, let them do the dirty jobs as well, let us have dust ladies as well as lady vicars. *Time* magazine has already written about a team of women furniture removers who call themselves the Mother Truckers.

In return, men must storm the bastions of femininity. Why shouldn't men go camping with Brown Owl and the Guides, why should they be excluded from Ladies Only carriages and the changing room at Biba's? Why can't men be nuns, and chorus girls and principal boys? Why can't they spread themselves luxuriously across the gatefold of *Playboy*?

The discrimination against men starts in the nursery, when they are barred from playing with dolls on the stupid pretext that if they do, they won't want to play with dollies when they grow up.

Why can't men come out (of anything except pubs) and go to Queen Charlotte's Ball dressed in white, and have the chance of being named Deb of the Year?

But Men's Lib aims to change more than this. In future when men leave school, they will be able to stay at home and do the flowers. They won't ruin their looks on their wedding day because they stayed up half the night before at some awful stag party, nor rupture themselves lugging their brides over the threshold.

In the new Masculine Utopia, a man will no longer have to bear the strain of supporting a wife and children on his own, which means that men will live longer. Let us fight for equal opportunities, ulcers and coronaries for women.

Men will also feel free to be kept by women and accept mink jackets and crocodile-skin briefcases. Nor will there be any stigma attached to the word househusband. While their wives go out to the top jobs, men will stay at home, have jollies with the milklady, go to Tupperware parties and gossip for hours to their men friends about getting the family whites whiter. Later they can serve up vats of baked beans to hungry children with appalling table manners who will all agree that Father knows best.

In the evening, after the children are tucked up in bed, the househusband will curl up in front of the electric logs, flick through a copy of *Man and Home* and wait for his lady and mistress to come home. Later, in bed, he won't be expected to take the sexual initiative, he can just shut his eyes, lie back and think of Charlton Athletic.

The househusband may fret occasionally about being

confined to 'unpaid domestic servitude'. But at least he won't have to suffer the terrible boredom of a nine to five job, nor the horrors of commuting, trapped like a sardine in the Tube, nor crawling at a snail's-pace up a motorway. Make Jam not Traffic Jams is the cry of the men of tomorrow.

Another of Men's Lib's aims is to free a man from paying unnecessary alimony. If on the other hand his rich tycoon of a wife runs off with her male secretary, she will be expected to support her husband in the style to which he is accustomed.

Women's Lib in America are battling to change words like boycott to girlcott, and history to herstory. Fight back, chaps, what about all those words which throw opprobrium on the male sex: MENace, MENdacity, MENtal, MENial, MEN-opause, MENstruation, to name only a few. Let us get Hi-Jack changed to Hi-Jill.

Literature, too, is hopelessly loaded against men. No one has ever written a classic about the gigolo with the golden heart. Nursery rhymes are even worse: dreadful allegations about little girls being made of 'sugar and spice and all things nice', while little boys are entirely composed of 'slugs and snails and puppy dogs' tails'.

Men may ask: what can I do about Men's Lib? The movement must be given exposure. On Women's Lib Day this year, women hurled their bras and cosmetics into dustbins as symbols of sexual oppression. On Men's Lib Day, I implore you to go out in the streets, throw away your belts, your braces and your Y-Fronts – and see what happens.

4 A Day's Hunting

My attitude towards blood sports is totally irrational. I detest otter and stag hunting. Beagling is far too energetic. Shooting involves too much time shambling about in silence and damp heather, and the only time I went to a bullfight I was so appalled I was sick on a black mantilla.

I must confess, however, that I have a sneaking fondness for fox hunting. I excuse my predilection by telling myself that foxes are vermin and they would have to be shot if they weren't hunted. I have a feeling that people get steamed up about fox hunting because foxes are so beautiful, and if it were a question of chasing snakes or rats down a sewer the anti-blood-sports brigade wouldn't be nearly so clamorous.

I also suspect a touch of class warfare; hunting is popularly seen as an upper-class sport, practised by the rich and seemingly arrogant. It would be more honest to call the dissenters the Anti-Blue-Blood-Sports Brigade.

Not that I was any good at hunting myself, being shunted out at the age of eight on a souped-up polo pony, who either bolted or lashed out at everything in sight. Seedlings trembled, hounds cringed at my approach, and most of the day was spent being sworn at by irascible farmers. But it was part of the stoicism of being a horsy little girl that one never let on how terrified one was.

On one occasion I even got a brush. My pony bucked me off at the first covert, and by the time I had caught the beastly thing half an hour later, hounds had run full circle and I was able to nip in at the kill and pretend I had been with them all along.

What really appealed to me was the glamour, and they are

glamorous those gaudy desperadoes in their pink coats, and those girls with their avocado-pear-in-the-mouth voices and faces straight out of *Country Life* – and how beautiful they looked hurtling across country as though they had a spare neck in their pockets.

I also have a horrified fascination for the ruthless single-mindedness of hunting people. Not far from the truth is that *Punch* joke:

First Rider: Who's that lying in the ditch?
Second Rider: Looks like the parson.
First Rider: Well leave him there, he won't be needed until next Sunday

Recently I accepted an invitation from David Sandeman, Master of the Crawley and Horsham, to attend their opening meet. 'Do you want a mount,' he said. 'No thanks awfully,' I said, 'I've a much better seat on a motor car these days.'

Hounds met at Knepp Castle in Sussex, and every living thing seemed to have turned up to give them a send off: men in anoraks weighed down by cameras, endless yapping dogs straining at their leads, ponyless girls in jodhpurs, Thelwell ponies sweating in their winter coats, older riders with faces red-veined like road maps. A nun went by in a wheel chair, her feet wrapped in polythene like a rose bush.

The meet had been arranged to coincide with half term at Eton. 'Is Miranda mounted?' shouted one chinless wonder to another. 'Far too often' came back the reply.

A large grey mare forgot herself enough to wolf half a dozen sandwiches on a silver salver. There was a lot of chat about tiger traps and half couples.

Several glasses of port later, the hunt moved off, surging out from the dark battlements into the most perfect autumn in years. No frost had yet ripped the leaves from the trees, and they glowed in the full glory: orange, crimson and saffron against a pewter grey sky.

I followed in the Land-Rover with Fred Mills, the Secretary of the Footfollowers Club, at the head of a gleaming crocodile of cars, everyone anxious to see some sport. In fact we saw nothing all day. The Crawley and Horsham ought to be renamed the Very Quickly and Horsham – they found a fox almost immediately, hounds and riders plunged into the amber gloom of the woods, and that was the last we saw of them.

The rest of the day was spent somewhat hilariously hunting the Hunt. The Land-Rover rolled over the fields like an Atlantic liner, but where it couldn't go, we walked, tramping down bridle paths, knee deep in mud, squelching through puddles and pig midden. I discovered that my new boots leak.

Every so often a felt-hatted woman would charge up to us braying, 'Where can we go to see something, Fred?' Every so often we would hear the tender melancholy note of the horn mocking us, and we would charge to the top of the hill, only to discover the hounds had run in the other direction.

The members of the Footfollowers Association were smashing – as though the Archers were for real after all, with sets by Lionel Edwards. We ate blackberries, and discussed ploughing marathons and mangelwurzels.

Finally having climbed every mountain, crossed every stream, we heard the long sad cry of the huntsman's horn calling it a day, echoing through the fading afternoon. Then the whole hunt came spilling past, tired horses, their legs stiff with mud, hounds still jolly, their tails wagging, riders lighting cigarettes and kicking their feet out of the stirrups.

The gorgeous Mr Sandeman slid off his huge horse. 'Not a bad day,' he said. 'We had some pretty good runs, didn't manage to kill any foxes though.'

Home they went to their hot baths, boiled eggs and stiff whiskies.

Pink in the face, exhausted but happy, I caught a train back to London and discovered that the quickest way to have a compartment, nay a whole wagon, to oneself is to travel with pig manure on one's boots.

Next day, however, I was still wondering why they hadn't caught any foxes. 'Oh,' said a friend, 'they've all moved into the suburbs, and a lot of them are living on Hampstead Heath and Barnes Common.'

Sure enough, when I looked in the E–K Directory, I found eight columns of Foxes.

5 Rugger à la Française

My hand is shaking so much I can hardly write, empty bottles litter the garden, records lie like a handful of loose change on the carpet, and if anyone's found a pram between Fulham and the City I'd be grateful if they'd let me know.

A three-day Bacchanalia has just ended. My husband's rugger club were playing host to a team from the French Vendée and their forty-one supporters, and despite present diplomatic hostilities, the *entente* couldn't have been more cordial.

When I originally heard we were putting up two Frenchmen, I was extremely tight-lipped. Our house is overcrowded anyway, and I had heard depressing stories about earlier French tours. 'Don't expect huge men with bedroom eyes and thighs like champagne bottles, talking about Proust and kissing your hand every five minutes,' said one wife sourly. 'They're all peasants and knee-high to a grasshopper.'

To my amazement, however, my husband arrives from Gatwick with two of the best-looking Frenchmen I've ever seen: Antoine, long-legged and exactly like Alain Delon, and Jules, who has sleepy yellow eyes and white teeth flashing above a dark red beard.

They have obviously been drinking since they left the Vendée, and the fact that it's my birthday gives us all *carte blanche* for a good deal of kissing. From then on they take to London as unhesitatingly as English spinsters take to the Costa Brava.

We only have time to open the whisky bottle and exchange a few laboured pleasantries, before the door bell rings. There has been a muddle and Ton-Ton, another Frenchman, has arrived also expecting to stay with us. He has a beige suit and face, a white polo-neck sweater and looks very King's Road. The other two obviously don't like him.

Antoine is now drinking neat gin. His eyes are beginning to cross and his leg is pressing against mine – so I ask him about his wife. He immediately produces a snapshot of a girl wearing a white peaked cap, spectacles and sneakers, and I lamely say she looks *très intéressante*. Jules is playing 'Mountain Greenery' on the piano. Ton-Ton is taking a colour photograph.

More Frenchmen and their English hosts arrive for supper. Everyone gesticulates a great deal and bares their teeth like a toothpaste commercial. My husband bears off a posse of Frenchmen to buy fish and chips, Antoine has switched to liqueur brandy in a beer mug and has cornered a nervous-looking wife.

The posse returns. My husband is crying with laughter. Three elderly Salvation Army ladies, one carrying a tambourine, had evidently rounded the corner just as the Frenchmen were relieving themselves against the Baptist Hall.

Everyone except Antoine, who is being sick upstairs, tucks into fish and chips. More colour photographs are taken. People are beginning to sing and throw grapes at each other. Jules and Ton-Ton disappear upstairs to be sick. Antoine reappears and makes a bee-line for our lodger who has just arrived. Then he sees her boyfriend is 6 ft. 2 in. and looks like a Luftwaffe pilot and goes briskly into reverse.

The party breaks up and everyone goes to bed. Then two pretty girls arrive from another party and everyone gets up again and the party goes on in the kitchen until four in the morning.

At last silence falls, followed by piercing shrieks. Antoine is assaulting our lodger and has to be forcibly removed. Silence falls again, followed by more shrieks: Ton-Ton has been pounced on by our senior cat.

At seven next morning, when baby demands breakfast, I comfort myself that the French will have such debilitating hangovers that they won't surface until lunchtime. Alas, there is Antoine – immaculate in a pearl-grey suit and basket-weave shoes – pale but ready for action. Five minutes later the others follow.

Last night's invasion has exhausted the coffee and bread supplies and no shops will be open for two hours, so everyone eats Stilton on digestive biscuits. Ton-Ton spends the next two hours taking colour photographs of me cleaning the bath, of my husband paying the milkman, of us both emptying a dustbin. Jules reads a comic, Antoine reads his passport.

The rest of the week-end passes in a dream. That night Antoine picks up a typist from Chigwell, who carries three changes of clothes in a paper bag ('You never know who you maight meet'). She misses her last train and stays the night.

Next morning we are up by nine drinking black velvet, and in the afternoon the French trounce my husband's team forty-three points to eight.

After *le match* there is *thé dansant*, which merges into a buffet supper and more *dansant*. Later, in deference to the Vendée supporters, the juke box is turned off and a muscular lady supporter in orange frills plays 'Le Tango Bleu' on the piano. Then she plays 'The Sound of Music', and suddenly everyone is doing the foxtrot like a social in Aberystwyth.

'What do you do for a labour?' one supporter asks me. I tell him, and then he tells me he is a student and very keen on English historians. 'I once 'ave the honour,' he says proudly, 'to meet your own A. J. B. Taylor in the Island of Wight.'

The French scrum-half passes out, and his friends wheel him round in our pram. It seems too funny to watch very carefully where they are taking him.

There is no point in going to bed and at 6.30 a.m. we bid our three Frenchmen a tearful farewell at Victoria. As they reel down the platform arm in arm, Antoine peels off to chat up a girl sitting on her luggage.

'French rugger players are so much better on their handling,' says my husband.

6 The Glamour of Doctors

People are fascinated by all things medical – you have only to listen to the relish in a woman's voice when she tells you she's 'under the doctor' or try to check a member of the prolapse-tariat once they're launched on their operation saga. But what is the reason for this fascination?

And why the adulation of the doctor himself? So he's a fine member of society and doing a grand job – but so are solicitors and tax collectors. This doesn't explain why nine out of ten heroes in romantic fiction are doctors, or the popularity of programmes like 'Dr Kildare' and 'Emergency-Ward Ten'. And why not 'Carry on Dentist' or 'The Flying Oculist'?

Is it because doctors deal with the fundamental problem of life and death, which is something we all have a stake in; or because sick people are vulnerable, and therefore susceptible to anyone who can bring them reassurance; or that the doctor – as someone who will listen to one's troubles – has largely taken the place of the parish priest?

Probably it's a combination of all these things. But my theory is that, to women, the answer is mostly sexual. The fascination of doctors is that they are the only people, apart from your husband if you've got one, who have legitimate access to your body – who are, in fact, licensed to grope.

You have only to take the recent court case of the man who went round the council estates knocking on housewives' doors saying he was a doctor from the council come to examine them. It worked like a charm – they all let him in.

Or the friend of mine – a very attractive man, used to a great deal of attention – who went to a party where no one was taking any notice of him. He turned to a girl and told her quite untruthfully that he was a gynaecologist. Her face lit up and she drew nearer. Warming to his subject he explained he was visiting England with a distinguished American colleague for the International Fertility Conference. He believed they had made a major breakthrough.

From that moment he was mobbed. All the women crowded round him, bombarding him with questions. One pretty girl insisted that he came upstairs and examined her. Two journalists interviewed him, and a TV producer offered him air space.

At school, where the only men we saw were the gardeners or the vicar, who sang castrato, we were all deeply in love with the school doctor and would try anything – blotting paper in our shoes, thermometers on our hot-water bottles – to gain admittance to the 'San'. One girl ate green apples to be able to complain of a stomach ache. She was horrified to find herself borne off to the cottage hospital where her appendix was removed.

However, not everybody sees doctors through rose-coloured spectacles. My husband once visited a woman doctor for an agonizing septic foot. She kept him waiting an hour, told him he should wash his socks more often, and then wrote him out a prescription for a bandage.

And a friend of mine, who went into a hospital to have her baby, was horrified to see protruding from the pocket of the doctor who was to handle the birth a booklet entitled *Introduction to Gynaecology*.

A ravishingly pretty girl I know, who was admitted to a South London hospital for an obstetrical operation, found to her intense embarrassment that the house surgeon arrived to examine her every day accompanied by a host of 'students'. It was only after she left that she learnt it wasn't a teaching hospital.

I know I should be more grateful to the medical profession. But the truth is that like all people blessed with excellent health, I am simply terrified of doctors.

Before visiting the doctor I always buy a completely new set of underwear and spend hours scrubbing myself. Then there's the horror of sitting in the waiting room, suffocating from the smell of disinfectant, trying to concentrate on colour supplements with all the best bits torn out, while some child with impetigo crawls all over you.

And when you actually see the doctor, what does he write on his little card as you laboriously describe your symptoms?

A friend of mine took a look at her card when the doctor was called to deal with some domestic crisis. Afterwards she told me: 'It said I was "bright-eyed, clear-skinned, slightly overweight and garrulous". What's garrulous, darling?' 'I think it's a kind of scurvy,' I said.

7 Bores and Boredom

My husband says I've got one of the lowest thresholds of boredom he's ever come across. I'm reduced to a state of actual physical pain by long car journeys, evenings at the ballet, parties where no one's taking any notice of me, dinner parties we're giving so I can't get out a book, all sport, all current affairs and anything factual on television.

It's the same with people. A man who bores me to death seems to fascinate other people. 'You ought to get him on to his own subject,' they cry. 'He's electrifying on ball bearings or chicken sexing.'

I'm bored too by people who tell me the plots of films, or the books they're reading, particularly when they read me long extracts. I glaze when people talk at length about their holidays – 'We found this marvellous little place on the N7, didn't look much from the outside' – to the fumbling counterpoint of snapshots.

I find resistance coming down like a steel trap when anyone gets on to stocks and shares, or sailing, or good wine, or even worse: cars. I run a mile if I see a man with holes in the back of his gloves.

Bores take me literally when I say: 'How are you?' and spend the next half hour taking me down every tube of their latest operation. Bores tell me incessantly about their children and, even worse, their crushed childhood.

Nothing is more boring than two men who were at school together: 'Remember Davenport Hicks?'

'J. J. or C. R. F?'

'Oh, J. J. of course, C. R. F. was a bit after my time. J. J.

achieved the glory of rowing for Oxford, and spent the rest of his life in exhausted mediocrity.'

And lovers too. All the world may proverbially love them, but they paralyse me. It's all right the first time, but after five lunch hours and it's still: 'Gideon says I've got such a pretty laugh (tinkle, tinkle). Yes, spaghetti and treacle pudding for me. Gideon says I could put on a fraction of weight. Have you noticed how his nose crinkles when he sneezes? You'll never guess what he said to me last night.'

It's even worse when it breaks up – with telephone calls at two o'clock in the morning. 'Since you were in at the beginning, I knew you'd want to hear the latest development. Gideon hasn't rung. Should I ring him and check his telephone?'

I know I myself am a terrible bore about the cats and having too much work to do. My husband says I bore for Fulham and the home counties when I don't know what to wear, or get on to the 'he said, she said, I said' syndrome.

But the professional yawn-maker is boring all the time. He's the kind of person who halts in full flow, scoops up a fistful of olives and says: 'Where was I?' and you haven't a clue.

Such practised bores often disarm you with flattery: 'You're such a good listener, I must tell you.' Or, 'You know all about this Johnnie Freud, don't you? Well, what do you make of this dream I had last night?' Or the honest 'I'm afraid I'm going to bore you', which entitles them to an hour's rabbiting.

Watch for the decorating bores. 'We want your advice about doing up the house,' they say. They don't. They want an excuse to wave thousands of nasty pieces of wallpaper in front of me, so I have to think hard deciding which one they've chosen.

Bores, like Eeyore, never stop grumbling: they have the worst headaches, the rudest taxi-drivers, the most disgusting foreign loos.

Bores are sad people, the deserted, those on the brink or in the throes of a nervous breakdown, the lonely who clutch your arm like the Ancient Mariner, the shy who are so scared of speaking that once started they go on like a three-wheel car on a tram line.

Bores come to drinks at 6.30 p.m. and are still there at midnight when your stomach is rumbling like Vesuvius, whereupon they cry blithely: 'Knowing how strong your drinks are, we took the precaution of having high tea beforehand.'

How do you shift them? My father, who's a pragmatist, turns off the light and plunges everyone in darkness. My husband switches off the heating or, in desperation, asks them to go.

Finally there are the public bores. My team of top drags would be headed by Mary Whitehouse and would include Julie Andrews, Vanessa Redgrave's baby, Mick Jagger, the Pope, Ian Paisley, Harold Wilson, Edward Heath, Jeremy Thorpe, Simon Dee, Christian Barnard, Noddy, Barbara Cartland, Bernadette Devlin, Ian Smith and Chairman Mao.

But then I'm bored by all Scotsmen, Welshmen, Irishmen, squatters, people who live in the country, people who live in the town, sailors, astronauts and pilots and the entire Kennedy clan. The only people who don't bore me are my son, who can't talk yet, and my husband – and he's pretty tedious when he gets on to the evils of mass media or river pollution.

Right, you can wake up now, I've finished.

8 Losing Face

I was sitting in the car with a teenage friend the other day, when a girl in a green shift and long blonde hair sauntered by.

'She's pretty,' I said, thinking narcissistically that she looked faintly like me.

'If you like that sort of thing,' said my teenage friend, shifting her chewing gum to the other side of her mouth.

'What sort of thing?' I demanded.

'Oh, those draggy clothes and that old-hat make-up. I mean, no one looks like that any more.'

I digested this and craned my neck to look in the driving mirror. Was I out of date, too? Did no one look like me either? I picked up the evening paper when I got home and found a feature on eye make-up. 'This is the face of 1971,' said the headline. 'Lashings of false eyelashes but chuck out that eye-liner.'

Charming, thought I. Eye-liner is the only thing that transforms my eyes from very piggy to not so piggy, and the only time I wore false eyelashes one of them fell off during dinner, and my host stamped on it, thinking it was an insect.

After a night of brooding, I rose early and took a bus to the West End. In Harridges windows were large notices announcing: 'Monsieur Claude Duval, the expert international beautician, is over for a week from France to give free advice on make-up and introduce his new range of cosmetics.' That's my boy, I thought.

M. Claude turned out to be a miracle of rare device in lilac suiting, with fixed velvety eyes, white hands that drooped like snowdrops and a rose-petal complexion. A crowd of women

34

shoppers, resting their swelling ankles, were watching him at work.

'Remove Madame's make-up,' he told a minion as I settled into the dentist's chair. When all traces of the face of 1960 had been removed, he peered at me through a magnifying glass and gave a deep sigh – the sort of sigh that Hercules might have given when first confronted with the Augean stables.

'Madame's skin has been totally neglected,' he said.

Starting to weed my eyebrows ferociously with a pair of scissors, he regaled his enraptured audience with a list of my imperfections.

There were red veins, open pores, whiteheads. Madame also had a combination skin, and to deal with both oily patches and ultra-dry patches she would need entirely different kinds of cleansing cream, moisturizers, toning lotion, skin food, night cream, morning cream, etc.

The minions bustled round assembling bottles on the counter. Madame, M. Claude went on, would also need anti-wrinkle cream for beneath her eyes, and soothing lotion for puffy eyelids. Madame had problem hair too, greasy with a trace of dandruff. She must have medicated lotion.

There were now enough bottles on the counter to open a chemist's shop. Was it necessary to buy all of them? I asked nervously. M. Claude was horrified. What was the point of his giving me free advice, if I didn't buy any of his products? My skin was in a very serious condition. Did I want to look like an old woman by the time I was thirty-five?

'It is very difficult,' he told his audience with a sigh, 'to paint over an imperfect surface.' He started painting huge circles round my eyes, dark blue, now yellow – 'to reflect the yellow in madame's eyes' – now pink, now white.

Why hadn't he perfected a lacquer that would spray an expression of permanent amiability on to the face, I suggested. He didn't like that. 'Close the mouth,' he interrupted sourly, starting to paint my lips.

Finally, after my 'ruddy' complexion had been toned down with a thick layer of green face powder, I was allowed to look at myself in the glass. At last, the face of 1971! I gave a wail of dismay. With my rouged cheeks, carmine lips and rainbow-coloured eyes, I looked like an old tart who'd been in a punch-up.

'Wonderfully soft effect,' chorused the minions, totting up my purchases. They came to £18·50. As I gasped with horror, M. Claude muscled in. Bearing in mind the condition of madame's skin, he said, she had spent ridiculously little.

Oh hell, I thought, it's the end of the month. I could pay by cheque, said one of the minions, if I had identification.

I produced my passport, which she studied for a minute. 'It doesn't look like Madame,' she said suspiciously.

It wasn't. In my haste to sneak out of the house, I'd mistakenly picked up an old passport belonging to my husband's first wife. So they had to make do with a crumpled reminder from the Gas Board.

I staggered home with my carrier bag, waiting for a chorus of approving wolf-whistles. They didn't come. One woman I know quite well cut me dead in the street. This is the face of 1971, I told myself firmly, it'll take some getting used to.

My husband didn't recognize me when he came to the door. He assumed that expression of bright insincerity with which he greets demands for jumble or complaints about rubbish being thrown over the wall. But, slowly, an expression of horror spread over his face. 'My God, it can't be,' he said. 'What have they done to you? Will it come off?'

My teenage friend came into the hall. 'You look like a dress rehearsal for the end of the world,' she said.

'It's the face of 1971,' I faltered.

'Well, roll on 1972,' said my husband.

9 Not Cricket

'Come back, Gideon, Daddy's not really being kicked to death, it's only a game, and don't suck those oranges, Samantha, they're for the players. I know it's cold, darlings, I'm cold too, let's walk round the pitch once more.'

The voice of the Rugger wife is heard in our land – but not for much longer. The season's nearly over, and soon enthusiastic husbands will be off to the nets every night, getting out of shape for the cricket season.

In theory, cricket should be a much better bet for the wife than Rugger – no more muddy boots in the washing-up bowl, no more unwashed kit discovered weeks later mouldering in the best suitcase, no more husbands with black eyes to set the neighbours talking, no more clutching warm half pints, wondering whether to look shocked when the Rugger Songs strike up.

Shivering on the touchline, she dreams nostalgically of sunny cricketing days among the buttercups, the ground spreading smooth and green like a giant billiards table, mulberries dropping on to the parked cars, smiling yokels propped on the gate. Like having babies, she forgets in between times what hell the cricket season is.

One problem is that, in our vile English climate, rough winds not only shake the darling buds of May, but of June, July, August and September as well. Time and again last year, it was up with the lark for a drive eighty miles across country to find the pitch under water. Other days were spent scuttling in and out of the pavilion to avoid the deluge.

There is, too, the nightmare of doing the teas – roping in

the reluctant spreaders, desperately uncurling the sandwiches, working over the bought cake to make it look home-made. And, with galloping inefficiency, I buy either too little – and have to divide, in true Galilean fashion, a couple of seedcakes between fifty people – or too much – and we live off sandwich spread for breakfast for the next six months.

There are all those extra shirts to wash: my washing is the kind that forces grey in – and beside the snowy whiteness of the other players my husband always looks like the fall guy in the Persil ads. And there are the flannels one forgets to collect from the cleaners.

And how about those fearsome lavatories? – corrugated hovels either buried deep in the stinging nettles, or else backing on to the men's loos, so one can hear the shy youth one has heroically been trying to 'bring out' for the past hour, boasting to the man in the next stall that he's got a pushover here.

Then, of course, there are the other wives – cricket seems to spawn a particularly grim collection – and girlfriends. Alas, it is always the biggest bitches whom the men love most. 'I was the first person to bring old Sue up here,' they claim. 'Then she took up with Mike, and then she moved on to John – and now she's marrying old Giles. She's an absolute sweetie, you know?'

But Sullivan's girlfriend capped them all. Sullivan was a young man with sticking-out ears, who was playing a trial game for the Free Foresters. With him was a fat girl in scarlet strap-under trousers, who kept up a running commentary on the game:

'Do look, Sullivan's fielded a ball. Now he's been moved to silly mid-on. Now he's straightening his cap. Oh, look, he's taken off his sweater, perhaps he's going to bowl . . . no, he isn't. Don't you think he's handsome?'

'Yes, in a way,' I said cautiously, 'but as long as you think so, that's the main thing.'

'Oh, Sullivan's chewing a piece of grass, and now he's watching a pigeon. I wish your last man would get out, or Sullivan's never going to get a knock. Oh, he's looking in this direction. Coo-ee! Sullivan!'

Eventually Sullivan got his knock, and made a spirited single before he was clean bowled to the noisy chagrin of his beloved. Later he consumed a great quantity of beer, and took to the woods with the wife of the man who bowled him.

Cricket is not all gloom and despondency. There are occasional heatwaves, there are manic days when one's husband makes runs, and some teams are definitely more amusing to play against than others.

The Army can be relied on to provide good food, impeccable manners and charming extrovert dogs. The Household Brigade, in particular, is always good for a giggle. Last year, there was a languid major who, whenever he failed to stop a ball, which happened frequently, turned to the man fielding next to him, and rapped out: 'Fetch it, Corporal.'

First prize for loveliness, however, goes to the Wine Trade, with their handsome dissipated faces and their crates of free drink. Sabotage is rampant, everyone gets tight at lunchtime.

The Wine Trade captain, a tawny giant, went in first after lunch and was bowled first ball. As he returned, the next man in asked him: 'What sort of ball was it?'

'I think it was a red one,' came the reply.

10 Come on Friday
if you Can

I hate going away for the week-end – like the mandrake, I scream when I'm uprooted. The trouble is I accept invitations months ahead in the hope that some cataclysm – an earthquake or a world war – will turn up to prevent us going. But the weeks melt away and suddenly it's Friday – and there's nothing to be done except pack and bear it.

My packing is frightful – a fierce challenge to the most crease-resistant material – and as I pack for every emergency, we usually need a removal van. Then there's the palaver of finding a baby-sitter for the cats, who work up a mammoth sulk unless they have someone living in.

There is, too, the inevitable row because we should have left at 4.30 to avoid the rush hour, and it's 5.30 and the windows still aren't shut and no one has written a *billet doux* to the milkman.

Invariably the first five miles are punctuated with cries of 'Oh God!' as I remember things left behind. So we plunge back and forth doing U-turns against the ever-increasing traffic to pick up the Cow and Gate, turn off the oven or tear my underclothes from the line.

We've suffered some harrowing week-ends in our time. There was one house where children and animals ran amok and meals turned up burnt and five hours late. There weren't enough blankets on our huge damp bed, we had to climb out to switch off the light, and our host kept coming in to collect socks and collar studs as our bedroom was his dressing room.

We staggered down to breakfast to find our hostess drying nappies under the grill, saying: 'Jennifer's found such a fun new game, cleaning between her toes with your electric tooth-brush.'

We spent an equally depressing week-end in a super-efficient house, where we didn't dare sit down for fear of rumpling the cushions, where mats with hunting scenes were slipped beneath our glasses in case we marked the table, and ashtrays disappeared every time a cigarette was flicked.

'I want you to lie in,' said our hostess, as we went to bed, but by nine in the morning, the smell of disapproval and frying bacon was drifting up from the kitchen. Every time we sallied forth with our sponge bags, the bathroom was occupied, until at 12 o'clock, our host tapped tartly on the door: 'Do be down by 12.30, the Smith-Jamesons are coming for drinks.'

Bad-tempered and unwashed, we went down to find the Smith-Jamesons were a couple of country smuggies, balancing on their heels in front of the fire. 'I suppose you come from Chelsea,' said Mrs Smith-Jameson, giving my husband's hair and our unkempt appearance an old-fashioned look. 'I couldn't live in London, such a dirty place.'

Something about other people's houses – probably not feeling free to raid the larder – makes one permanently hungry, hanging around for the next meal. In houses where we don't get enough to eat, my husband becomes terribly polite, leaping to his feet at the end of each course, pressing the hostess down with a heavy hand, saying: 'I'll clear away, you must have a rest.'

To get in on the act I generally grab the sauce-boat and follow him into the kitchen, to find him tearing strips off the leg of lamb like Henry VIII.

Not having enough to drink is almost as bad. We had barely been in the house of some friends five minutes before they told us they had given up alcohol for Lent. And they added ominously: 'We find the best way is to have no drink in the house.'

I am highly suspicious of week-ends in big baronial country houses – just look what happened to Duncan when he went to stay with the Macbeths. Last year, we had one very grand week-end. As soon as we arrived, a fleet of servants did an N K V D on our suitcases. Clothes were immediately removed, and I saw myself going down to dinner wearing only my pearls. When I came back from my bath, however, everything had been laid out on the bed, including the half-eaten apple I'd started in the car and shoved into my suitcase.

In the morning, my husband, unable to find his trousers and having failed to communicate with a Spanish maid in the corridor, pressed the nearest bell, which turned out to be a fire alarm.

One of our fellow guests kept on drinking, and disgraced himself: there was some trouble about his lurching into his hostess's bedroom in the middle of the night. When he appeared next morning, bleary, unshaven and in his pyjamas, dowagers swooned with horror – so he returned upstairs, shaved off his moustache and came down again. No one recognized him, and he was welcomed effusively.

It's bad enough dressing for dinner when one goes away. There are worse things, though – a friend tells of a terrifying wife-swapping week-end where everyone was expected to undress for dinner. But surely the most alarming of all week-ends is the summons to come and 'meet Mother'.

When I was eighteen, I fell in love with a man called James, who asked me to meet his family. From the moment I arrived, it was clear that his mother and I were doomed to mutual antipathy. She had small eyes and a mouth that shut like a steel trap.

Her worst suspicions seemed well founded when she discovered make-up on the towels, mascara on the pillows, and – when I got tar on my feet from the beach – cannibal foot-steps all over her white drawing-room carpet.

.The day I left, however, she obviously suffered from remorse and brought me breakfast in bed: herrings and oatcakes. As I can't eat herrings I tipped them down the loo. Alas, just as I was making my farewells, the loo overflowed, and in the flood of water that gushed into the passage, there were my breakfast herrings swimming for their lives.

11 Cooper's Alphabet of Clichés

A is for all right which it will be on the night, and for adopted children who grow so like their parents, and *The Archers*, which is so true to life, and Americans – I can't stand them as a race, but I like them individually and they're so good at remembering names.

B is for the boys you can't tell from the girls, and bulldogs who are surprisingly good with children, and beating which always hurts me more than it hurts you, and bullies who are such cowards at heart.

C is for the cruelty one has to resort to in order to be kind, and the Chinese who all look alike, and Chinese food – an hour after which you feel hungry.

D is for the Dunkirk spirit, and drinking at lunchtime which everyone claims they can't do, and this day and age, and Don Juans who are all latent homosexuals.

E is for exploring every avenue, and eggs being so versatile, and how exhausted one feels after that early night.

F is for fish and chips which taste so good out of newspaper, and fair enough, and far be it from me to, and forbidden fruit, and food which tastes so much better out of doors or when someone else cooks it.

G is for great minds thinking alike, and gentlemen who prefer blondes, and gardens which you should always have seen last week when the azaleas were out.

43

H is for hors d'œuvres – a meal in themselves, and anything home-baked being so much better than anything bought, and homosexuals who are all latent Don Juans, and *Hair* – I only went to hear the marvellous music.

I is for influence in high places, and illness which really takes it out of you, and the incurable laziness of the English working man.

J is for just a line to thank you and just good friends, and Jews who are among some of my very best.

K is for I don't know much about painting, but I know what I like, and those tins of Kit-e-Kat, which form the basis of curry in Indian restaurants.

L is for let's face it, and losing a son and not gaining a daughter, and lesbians – what on earth do they do ? – and long hair which I don't mind at all as long as it's clean, and the Labour Party which is growing so like the Conservative Party.

M is for mother who always knows best, and mongrels who are so intelligent, and Mr Right who takes his time to come along, and men, you want to watch the ones who don't have any men friends.

N is for newly washed hair which you can't do a thing with and nymphomaniacs who don't really enjoy it, you know, and North-country people who are so surprisingly hospitable.

O is for Oh, this old thing, when a dress is admired, and old age which is creeping up on us.

P is for pornography, so boring my dear, and our policemen so beloved of foreigners, and pigs who are really such clean animals, and pot which simply had no effect on me at all.

R is for reading – I never touch fiction any more, only biographies – and for red wine, which you don't *have* to have with steak, and for reformed whores, there's no prude like one.

S is for that schoolgirl complexion, and the ability to be silent together, which is always considered a test of true love, and for speaking more than three languages being proof of intellectual ability, and stuffing which is knocked out of you when you go to prep school, and scientists who are always described as brilliant to compensate for being unsmart.

T is for the theatre, which people in London never go to, and two people living more cheaply than one, and the thought that counts, and tunes which they don't write like that nowadays.

U is for ups and downs which everyone has, and ugly women who are always so grateful.

V is for a lovely speaking voice and violence – there's far too much on television.

W is for warm hands which reflect that cold heart, and Welshmen being such fine singers, and Wagner, who I've grown out of actually, I only listen to Bach.

X is for X who is helping the police with their inquiries, and for our digs on the holiday postcard.

Y is for you and yours, and you pays your money and takes your choice, and the years that go faster as you grow older.

Z is for zoo animals who are so much happier in captivity and for Zebra, Zanzibar, Zulu and all the other corny old words they put at the end of alphabets.

12 A Bitches' Inventory

The backbiter is the bitch I find the least lovable. She simultaneously puts you down, puts herself in a good light, and drops a third unfortunate right in it.

'Gideon said you weren't fit to eat with the pigs,' she begins blithely. 'But I stuck up for you. I said you were.' Or, 'When I said what a pretty girl you were, Gideon laughed so much, he nearly fell off the bar stool.'

And when you know you've behaved badly at a party, she's bound to say: 'All the other guests rang up to say how drunk you were. I must say I didn't notice a thing.'

The bubble-pricker is the bitch who waits until you're feeling really manic to say: 'I tried to find a moment all the way through dinner to tell you you'd got cabbage on your teeth, but you were so busy vamping that divine man.' Or when, after five gruelling interviews, you've landed a marvellous job she has great pleasure in telling you: 'Oh, you can't work there, the company's going bust any minute. That's why they're absolutely desperate for staff.'

The honest broker is one of the deadliest of the species. She manages to convince you she is doing you a marvellous turn by being honest.

Her technique is to demoralize you with an opening phrase: 'May I really be frank for once?' or 'As your closest friend, I feel it is my duty', or worse, the devastating: 'How tough are you?'

Then, shining with virtue, she moves briskly into the attack, announcing: 'Your feet smell', 'That new suit you spent a fortune on isn't really your colour'. Or (and this is the one she

46

really enjoys), 'Your husband made a fearful pass at me last night. Of course I was appalled and told him go and jump in the lake, but even so, sweetie, I'd never look you in the face unless I cleaned the slate between us.'

The gloom merchant is the bitch, who, however awful you are feeling, is guaranteed to make you feel worse. When you're just back from holiday, and deeply conscious of putting on weight, she will shout across a crowded room: 'Expecting a baby, darling?'

When you're feeling out of sorts, she immediately suggests you're starting the Change of Life, and even when you're looking your best she's certain to take you on one side and whisper: 'Don't you think you and I have got to the stage, darling, when mini-skirts and hair worn over the face look a tiny bit silly?'

Whenever she goes to a party she always routs out the girl with the most terrible legs, crying: 'What super stockings, everyone *do* look at Samantha's stockings.'

The backhander is the bitch who spreads gloom and despondency through the backhanded compliment. 'I wish I had your relaxed attitude,' she coos, lulling you into a sense of security, 'and could live in such a pigsty without it getting me down.' Another of her gay little asides is: 'Gosh, I envy your tiny bust, it must be so much easier for clothes.'

The twister is the bitch who turns all your remarks to her own advantage:

Me: I adore your dress.
Bitch: Yes, everyone does, I can never understand why.
Me: I did enjoy talking to your mother (turgid old crone).
Bitch: Yes, it's amazing how Mummy can get on with anyone.
Me: I do think your husband is attractive.
Bitch: He likes you too, tremendously, but he did say that physically you weren't really his type.
Me: I say, Gideon's just made a pass at me.
Bitch: He makes a pass at everyone. That boy's covered more sheet miles. . . .

The imperfect guest is the bitch who comes to dinner and instantly recognizes the unreal thing. 'Fake mashed potato,' she cries to all and sundry. 'How delicious, I can't think why

47

people get in such a tizzy over a few chemicals.'

If you give her pork, she immediately praises it to the heights and then asks for horseradish sauce. And having guzzled her way through five courses and a box of After Eight, she will turn to you, saying, 'Thank goodness you took me at my word and didn't go to any trouble.'

The bluff-caller is the bitch who knows instinctively that even though you are laughing like a hyena you haven't really got the point of the boss's last joke. She sidles up and says in a stage whisper, 'I missed that, do tell me why it was funny.'

The best bluff-caller of all was a very distinguished old lady I had tea with the other day, who had recently emerged from one of her periodic visits to a mental home. 'And how are your two little boys?' she asked me graciously. I decided to humour her: 'Very well indeed,' I said. 'Don't be silly,' she said icily, 'you know perfectly well you've only got one.'

13 Is it Time for a Degree in Sex?

Pondering rather gloomily this week on the merits of sex education for eleven-year-olds, I ask myself where's it all going to end? Will our children be taking sex at O-Level in a few years' time, with *Portnoy's Complaint* and *Lady C.* as set books? And how will they cope with their practicals? And will pupils who show no aptitude for sex have to give it up at thirteen?

Enough fuss, too, is made about public school boys having the edge over grammar school boys when it comes to landing the posh jobs. But imagine the furore when girls with first-class honours in sex keep getting promoted over rivals who can only boast a first in geography.

And consider the headaches of being a parent. If in future years I tick my son off for chatting up the girl next door all day, he'll just tell me he's doing his homework, or perhaps he'll turn accusingly to my husband and ask: 'What did you do in the sex war, Daddy?'

I begin to wonder how my generation ever managed without a proper sex education. I was lucky of course, I lived in the country and there were always foals being born and cows being mated. But I still got in a muddle: I couldn't sort out geldings and mules, and having read about racehorses like Blue Peter being at stud, I assumed for years that Stud must be the name of a very chi-chi Old Horses' Home.

Occasionally, when we were wandering round the garden, my mother, much embarrassed and frenziedly tugging off rose-heads, would try and tell me the odd fact of life. Usually I knew it already, and helped her along. A friend reported that when

49

her mother tried to tell her about sex she kept getting bits wrong.

Having devoured *Gone With the Wind* at an early age, I thought I knew all about pregnancy, and when I went away to school, my favourite game after lights out was to enact the birth scene from *Green Dolphin Country* with my friend Jennifer Snooky. One of us played the doctor, which only involved brow-mopping and tugging, and the other took the far more coveted part of the woman in labour, grunting and groaning so realistically that invariably the dormitory prefect woke up.

But if we knew how babies came out, we were very hazy about how they got in. We didn't get on to Reproduction until the Fifth Form, and even then they skated round the subject for weeks, telling us about saddles of worms, rabbits and fish eggs. Finally, on the week scheduled for human reproduction I caught chicken-pox, and by the time I'd recovered they'd moved on to reptiles, which perhaps accounts for my muddled thinking ever since.

My husband claims he first learnt about reproduction at prep school when his form were straggling along the sands one Sunday afternoon and suddenly a boy called Stuart piped up: 'I say, chaps, I know how babies are made.'

All around there were cries of: 'Go on, Stuart. Tell us.'

'The man lies on top of the woman,' said Stuart portentously, 'and is excused into her.'

Back at St Trinians, I remember, we learnt a bit from the Bible, Leviticus and Song of Solomon in particular. But we were totally mystified by homosexuals. Someone once asked our poor divinity mistress what Our Lord thought about them and she replied: 'He feels very sorry for them.' Which didn't get us much further.

What exactly had poor Oscar Wilde done? We gleaned inadequate information from Marlowe and stirring boys' school books like *The Hill* and *The Loom of Youth*. Chaucer, of course, taught us a lot about everything, so did Shakespeare, and we giggled like mad over a bowdlerized verions of *Othello* which changed strumpet to trumpet to produce the immortal line: 'She played the trumpet in my bed.'

Dictionaries were a dead loss. You looked up intercourse, it said coition; you turned to coition, it said intercourse. A prostitute was defined as a whore, a whore as a harlot, a harlot as a prostitute. How we went round the gooseberry bush.

First-aid books were more rewarding. You learnt about fringe subjects like emetics and bowels and venereal diseases, which I'd always thought were something you caught in the spring, tra-la. There was one splendid chapter on having a baby at home which made it sound just like a teenage fruit-cup party: 'Take two large jugs and a large enamel bowl.'

And yet, and yet, this feverish pursuit of sexual knowledge had nothing to do with love as it first struck me at the age of eleven. I fell deeply in love with a prefect called Angela Wallis who played third man at lacrosse and looked like Reggie Bosanquet. How chastely and undemandingly I adored her, giving her my sweet ration every month, filling her locker with bluebells in the summer and hazel nuts in the autumn.

The fact that she didn't deign to speak to me once in two years did nothing to diminish my passion, but at thirteen, feeling a guilty thrill of infidelity, I suddenly switched to men. In quick succession Budge Patty, Richard Todd, Brian Close, Louis MacNeice, John Carol Case became the object of my undying affection.

Often I cried myself to sleep at the sheer impossibility of any of them loving me back – but if Budge Patty or any of the others had actually turned up and tried to seduce me behind the squash courts, I should have died of horror and shame.

Obviously there is a divergence when one is eleven between theory and practice. But I find it sad that sex seems to be taught today with such earnestness and lack of humour, and everyone seems to have forgotten words like joy, magic, affection and – most important of all – love.

14 Alleluia

The leaflet through our letterbox announced a Divine Healing Crusade at our local hall, and promised 'genuine miracles of the Sixties'.

On one side of the leaflet were photographs of the Minister running the crusade and several people who claimed to have been cured by him. They included a doctor and a matron who had strings of letters after their names, but who didn't appear to exist when I checked with their medical councils.

On the other side of the leaflet was a drawing of a built-up shoe, with the caption: 'Shoe worn before being healed. The Minister prayed for me, I felt my leg lengthen, for it was two inches shorter than the other one. Both legs are now the same length.'

I arrived at one of the sessions to find the hall hung with bunting, and the Minister – looking older than his photograph – addressing a capacity audience. His voice was that refined camped-up North Country, often mistaken in the South for homosexual. He had the crowd eating out of his hand. One moment they were falling about with laughter, the next whipped up into a frenzy of 'Praise the Lords'.

Sitting behind him, idly flicking through a huge Bible, and glancing frequently at the clock, was one of the best-looking Negroes I've ever seen. On the Minister's left, never taking his eyes off him, sat a bored man with a mane of grey hair who let out the occasional 'Alleluia'. A woman in a black velvet fore-and-aft was playing the electric organ.

The audience were a mixed bunch. The front row were middle-aged women with parish hats and corrugated hair.

There was a sprinkling of coloured people, a few mothers with babies, a row of giggly teenage girls with long straggly hair, and half a dozen small boys who sat behind them and pinched their bottoms. In front of me, two youths sat holding hands.

The Minister was talking of his recent campaign: 'Mrs Bonce of Solihull,' he said, his voice growing husky with passion, 'was carried in bodily, was instantly healed and ran round the yard.'

'Alleluia,' cried the corrugated ladies.

'Carried in bodily was Mrs Bonce. Now she says every day is brighter.'

The teenage girls shook with suppressed giggles.

Above the platform hung a huge notice in red, orange and green saying: 'As many as touched Him were made whole.' He was evidently not the only one who was going to be touched – a collection came round. We were urged to give generously.

The Minister launched into a vigorous attack on the Health Service, cracked a few jokes and then became serious. Anyone who wished to be healed must raise their hands. Gradually about thirty were held up. A steward took their names and addresses while the Minister kept up a running commentary:

'Put up your hands. Praise be to Jesus, sign the cards, Praise the Lord, do help them sign – they may be in pain, wonderful Jesus, hand the cards to the stewards so we can keep in touch with you. Pray, when the time comes, that person about to be healed is your mother. Or your father, if it's a man,' he added hastily.

When we had finished a rousing hymn, the Minister came down from the platform and was joined by three henchmen. 'I want to start with the three people with thrombosis,' he said. A woman hobbled forward on crutches.

'Take your time, dear one,' purred the Minister, stroking her face. He put his arms round her and rocked her back and forth. She gave a gasp into the microphone and said the pain was gone. She told the audience her name and address, and said: 'I want you all to know, I've been healed, I've been three years walking with a stick.'

'Off you go then, round the hall,' said the Minister, and she stumped along, with 'Praise the Lords' on all sides.

An arthritic case came forward and was sent back sharply. 'I'm only dealing with thrombosis at the moment,' snapped the Minister. Another thrombosis came up, the Minister put a double lock on her and said 'Heal, heal' into the microphone. The woman fainted into the arms of a henchman who laid her on the floor.

Next the Minister cured an angina case and sent her running round the room. 'You can't run with angina, friends,' he told the audience.

Soon she was lapping the thrombosis victim, who was still stumping round muttering 'Praise the Lord', but was in turn lapped by a small boy cured of asthma.

They were coming up thick and fast now. Clinch, 'heal', collapse into the henchman's arms; clinch, 'heal', collapse; clinch, 'heal', collapse. The bodies were laid out side by side. The front of the hall resembled Hyde Park in a heatwave.

One man limped up and limped down again uncured. A woman was told to throw away her crutches and fell over. 'Close your eyes and think of Jesus,' the Minister said tartly to a girl lying adoringly at his feet.

A fat woman lying beside her suddenly shouted: 'I'm floating on air. I want to sing Onward Christian Soldiers.' And she did – moving discordantly from key to key while the congregation struggled to keep up.

Then, gradually, the prone filed back to their seats, the Minister returned to the platform and the meeting ended with a hymn and a prayer. As the Minister walked out of the hall, he seemed reduced in stature, a little man with tired shifting eyes and a briefcase.

A woman rushed round giving addresses of people who'd been 'genuinely healed' that evening. One was a gentle, elderly spinster who lives with her budgerigar half a mile from me. She told me she was in constant pain.

'The hospital won't believe there's anything wrong with me, they keep sending me along to the psychiatric ward. I think that Minister is a good man. He didn't cure my pain, but he made my nervous headaches better. I'm going to several faith healers at the moment, but they cost a lot.'

All the lonely people, where do they all come from? I don't know, but a lot of them end up at Divine Healing Crusades.

15 The Dustbin Problem

Nothing is more depressing than returning from holiday. This year it was particularly traumatic because we'd left the baby behind for a week, and I was terrified he wouldn't recognize me. In the end it was me who didn't recognize him. Our baby-minder had stuffed him so full of goodies, he'd put on pounds; and his hair, which he normally wears in a straight blond Beatle cut, had been coaxed into a mass of dark Brylcreemed curls.

But it was bliss to see him, the house was still there, and all the cats were present if incorrect: three of the kittens had reached the age of puberty and had turned the back garden into a brothel. The post was fairly harmless too, bristling with final reminders, but no one had sacked us. What a painless homecoming, I thought smugly.

Next morning, I realized I'd forgotten to put out the dustbins before we went. When I opened the lid, I nearly fainted. Maggots! Millions and millions of them – I wouldn't have believed there were so many maggots in the world – and they'd started to crawl towards the house.

Whimpering with panic, I fled inside and told my char. 'Ring up the council,' she said. 'They'll be round to fermigate in a trice.'

So I rang the town hall and asked for the sanitary inspector. 'Public health inspector,' said the operator reprovingly and transferred me to every room in the building before getting the right department.

Having bleated out my story to three different people, I was put through to the man who deals with my district. He said I should ring the borough engineer and complain that my dust-bins hadn't been emptied.

'But they couldn't be emptied,' I protested. 'They weren't put out, and the next lot of dustmen. . . .'

'Refuse collectors,' he said reprovingly.

'. . . refuse collectors, don't come until Wednesday – by which time the maggots will have taken the place over.'

'Is the nuisance outside the premises?' he asked.

'I always keep the dustbin in the bedroom, particularly when it's full of maggots,' I said. 'Of course it's outside.'

'We can do nothing about it then,' he said triumphantly. 'We only tackle nuisances inside the house.'

'What about rats,' I said. 'When one of our neighbours had a plague of rats in his shed, they sent the rat catcher.'

'Rodent operative,' he said patiently. 'Maggots are different. I suggest you go out and buy some DDT or Jeyes and pour boiling water over them.'

I slammed the phone down, then rang again. 'Give me the maggot operative,' I said. The telephonist was not amused and gave me Mr Unhelpful again. 'If I bring the dustbin inside the house, will that alter the situation?' I asked.

'I've got better things to do than waste my time on minor nuisances,' he said.

'It's a large nuisance, and it's what I pay my rates for,' I said and rang off muttering.

Once again I met the baleful eye of my char: 'If Carol's mum had been treated like that,' she said, 'she'd be down the town hall breaking the place up by now.'

Now I don't know Carol's mum from Frankenstein, but I can tell when someone's calling me yellow. Taking a deep breath I rang my public health friend again. 'One of the maggots has crossed the threshold,' I said.

I heard him draw in his breath. 'They're on the move,' I went on, warming to my subject. 'They'll be using the telephone and drinking my drink in a minute.'

After that we had a slight ding-dong, and in the end I rang off defeated. To save face, I then rang the Ministry of Health, but their refuse department appropriately refused to do anything about it, and referred me to the town hall.

Disheartened, I set out to find some Jeyes. My favourite chemists were singularly frivolous about the whole thing: 'There's been a plague of maggots this year,' they said. 'We've run out of Jeyes. Why not hold on until the week-end, you'd make a bomb flogging them as bait to all the amateur fishermen round here.'

But I trudged on until I did finally track down some Jeyes. Rather to my annoyance, it did the trick.

16 Disastrous Dinners

I am not one of Nature's hostesses. Even though I start cooking and bulling up the house weeks before a dinner party, I am always beset by terrible disasters.

To begin with, you can never tell if your guests are going to get on. With the loveliest people, it can be instant hackles, and that conversation killing: 'Actually I don't agree', with the steely glint in the eye.

Sometimes they don't talk at all, and in a desperate attempt to spark off chatter, I make more and more fatuous remarks. Or almost worse, the two couples get on so well that my husband and I wonder if anyone would notice if we went to bed.

A great mistake is to crack up one lot of guests to the other. 'You're going to simply adore Gideon and Samantha!' They never do.

Guests to be avoided include:

The slow eater, who insists on telling long stories and finishing up all his food.

The non-eater, who pushes her food to the side of her plate after one mouthful and then blows cigar smoke over everyone.

The wife who rings up at the last moment, and says, 'Charles is hungover and won't come, may I bring my sister, it won't foul up your numbers will it?'

The couple who go to cocktail parties and arrive very drunk an hour and a half late when you've asked an ultra-respectable couple to meet them – then have a row, tell blue stories and fall asleep after dinner.

The bachelors who specially ask you to fix them up with a divine girl, and when you do, spend the entire evening chatting up all the married women.

The lovers who start patting each other's thighs at 9.30, whose eyes combine and turn soft at 9.40, and who are out of the house by 9.45.

The women your husband fancies. The only solution is to give them asparagus or sweet corn – no one looks sexy with butter running down her chin.

Our house is so difficult to find that people always arrive late, which means that by the time we go into dinner, I've had so many dry Martinis I'm practically under the piano, and it no longer seems to matter that I haven't put the potatoes on.

I get far too happy to remember where people are supposed to sit, so the guest of honour ends up with a kitchen knife and the side plate with rabbits round the edge that was meant for my husband.

Even if I stay sober, there are disasters. I forget about napkins and have to rush upstairs, yank them out of the laundry basket and then iron them on the floor. Or the baby decides to stub his banana out all over the carpet, as the doorbell goes.

Or the casserole turns over as I'm taking it out of the oven. Or the top of the pepper mill comes off and a shower of peppercorns cascades irretrievably into the goulash. Or the meat's tough, and I see everyone's jaws working desperately like cows chewing the cud. Or my husband starts offering everyone second helpings when there aren't any.

I forget, too, what I gave the same guests last time. 'Isn't Jilly's *pâté* heaven?' they say. 'Yes, every time I mean to ask her how she makes it.'

Once, when we were first married, we served what the butcher described as Manchurian partridges. They went so hard that every time we tried to carve them they shot across the room, like Hunka Munka's doll's-house food, and were finally even rejected by the cats.

Dining out I adore, but we do get ourselves into some terrible muddles. Time and again we've over-eaten our way through a whole shepherd's pie and the remains of Sunday's

60

rhubarb crumble, and are just loosening our belts when the telephone goes and an irate voice says: 'Aren't you coming?'

I can't say, like Maurice Bowra, that we're more dined against than dining, but I remember in the days when Robert Carrier was writing in the colour supplement we would often have last Sunday's *coq au vin* five days running in a variety of houses.

One of our dreads are those houses where we don't get enough to drink:

'We've become awfully fond of cider,' they say, pouring into eggcup-sized glasses, when my tongue is hanging out for a stiff gin. One soak I know, to guard against such circumstances, has deliberately established a reputation for incontinency so he can charge out of the room every quarter of an hour and have a swig of whisky from the flask in his coat pocket.

And then there are those terrifying grand dinners, when six people sit down at a table big enough for twenty, and one's platitudes have to carry across eight feet of polished mahogany.

I remember, too, when I was much younger, going to dinner with a very arrogant old lady who made me so nervous that, as soon as I sat down, I leapt to my feet saying: 'I hope I haven't taken your chair.'

'These are *all* my chairs,' she said icily.

17 Lunching Out

Lunching out is my third favourite pleasure in the world. Wriggling into my gladdest rags, shutting the front door on the chaos and the cats and sauntering forth to Soho to meet some lovely man.

I love the delicious jostle of the whole occasion; the jokes and gossip and gentle flirtation. Just the sight of a bottle of white wine gleaming like topaz in a bucket of ice gets me going; ah, the bliss of good food, rose-pink langoustine, mayonnaise glistening like buttercups, the dark beauty of roast duck, the scent of garlic and herbs.

I also adore watching other people in restaurants, beautiful people toying with steak tartare, hoping to be recognized, married couples eating but not talking, lovers eating each other, illicit couples ducking nervously behind the celery and the gristicks every time the door opens, children doing more whining than dining, storing food in the corner of their cheeks like cherubs at the corner of old maps, then suddenly spraying spinach all over the snow-white tablecloth.

I even love those dreadful seaside hotels where so many Sunday lunches are spent chatting up rich old aunts. My husband was once handed a typed menu in a Worthing hotel, which offered him 'Cream Passionel'.

Unable to face this, he asked the waiter what cheese they'd got. 'Both, sir,' said the waiter.

Or the cavalry officer friend of my father who was presented with a mound of stodge. 'What on earth's this?' he asked.

'Baroness pudding,' said the mess steward. 'God help the baron,' was the reply.

Phoney restaurants always make me giggle, the sort of place where the food takes longer to read about than eat, and which even goes into ecstasies over: 'A gleaming white bone china cup, filled with freshly brewed Kenyan coffee hidden by foamy mountains of rich fluffy cumulus clouds of whipped cream.'

Or those places where the *chat du jour* is more important than the *plat du jour*, and whenever you ask the head waiter what something is, he launches into a fifteen-minute eulogy.

There was the hilarious occasion when I lunched in one of those chi-chi Polynesian restaurants, and two of the crocodiles – part of the pseudo jungle setting – got locked in some priapic grapple. Such was the threshing that the RSPCA was summoned and a little man in gumboots had to thread his way through the packed tables and prise the crocodiles apart.

And one short-sighted chum, lunching in a fashionable Indian restaurant, thought the basket of hot flannels brought for her to wipe her hands on were some exotic Indian pudding, and forking them on to her plate, tucked into them.

Mind you, one can lunch with some problematic people. Another chum of mine went into a restaurant and ordered a huge carafe of whisky and drank the lot, and when she walked out quite vertically, all the waiters lined up and shook her by the hand.

Or there are meanies who say: 'I'm too exhausted to eat, but don't let that deter you.' So you timidly ask for the plainest omelette and a glass of water, whereupon their appetite promptly returns and they order smoked salmon and a vast T-bone steak.

There's also no getting away from the fact that lunch is a danger zone, the adulterer's launching pad. Because of the enforced discipline of having to go back to work or home to look after the children, you become far more forthcoming than you would if you had the whole afternoon free.

Intimacy begins as the first double gin and tonic bites an empty stomach, increases as the musky perfidious fires of the wine curl round inside you, and by the time you're swilling your third brandy, you've both earmarked that little hotel room with roses growing up the wallpaper where you're going to spend your first week-end together.

Fortunately, the spell is usually broken by those telling two minutes when with horribly flushed faces you emerge from the restaurant and confront one another in the glare of Shaftesbury Avenue, before you escape into the dim womblike friendliness of a passing taxi.

It's difficult to get away with anything, of course, in a village like Soho. I once lunched with a very dolly man who said he knew a little place 'where one never sees anyone who matters'. So round the corner we went to an Italian bistro that looked vaguely familiar.

On seeing us the head waiter turned green and sidled up to me. 'Meesis Cooper, I think I should tell you, Meester Cooper is lunching in the next room.'

Fortunately I had already told Meester Cooper I was out on the toot, but my lunch date was completely poleaxed.

18 Some Have Class

Unkind readers are always accusing me of being a snob. Now I think they're wrong. As I was only saying to Princess Anne the other day, some of my best friends are working class.

I admit I'm bored into the ground by twitchy little modern boys hawking the chips on their shoulders round in red spotted handkerchiefs like Dick Whittington. But that doesn't mean I'm a snob – I'm just as bored by a roomful of braying telegraph poles talking foxiana.

I was certainly a horribly snobbish child. I go hot and cold when I remember how we mobbed up one poor little girl called Jennifer Hogg because her father travelled in ladies' underwear. 'What does your father do, Hoggie?' we kept asking her. 'He's in the clothes line,' she used to say. 'Ha, ha, ha,' we would chorus. 'Hoggie's father hangs his mother on the clothes' line.'

But then my generation were obsessed with class. Our gods were Nancy Mitford and Evelyn Waugh. From the age of fourteen, we tremulously waited for Lord Right to come along.

We all learnt U-usage off by heart, and went round carefully calling week-ends 'Friday to Monday', trying to eat kippers with forks (fish knives were Non-U), and never taking anyone home to tea, in case Mummy poured the milk in first.

Today's younger generation, of course, have gone to the other extreme. They're so determined to break down the class barriers, that they don't acknowledge class exists at all. As soon as they leave Eton or wherever, they assume a flat classless accent.

Nevertheless, it doesn't stop the hypocrisy. 'We've got such

an amusing couple to meet you,' cries the hostess. 'Real
people, so genuine and natural. He's very outspoken, and she
wears some rather bizarre clothes, but I think it's so important
to widen one's circle of friends, don't you agree.' What she
means is that they're as common as muck, and she wants you
to know she's not unaware of the fact, but to commend her
lack of snobbery at the same time.

Mind you, I'm a raging hypocrite too. How the plum in my
mouth grows when I'm talking to someone grand on the telephone. How often have I claimed intimate friendship with
some celebrity I've only read about in the gossip column.

But I think it would be a tragedy if class disappeared altogether, because it's such a giggle. My daily woman was grumbling the other day because her daughter never came to see
her any more. 'She's got so la-di-da since she married into the
professional classes,' she said darkly. 'What does her husband
do ?' I asked. 'He's an undertaker,' she said.

And one can get in such a muddle. My mother was recently
at a very grand dinner. 'Do you know Bolton?' one old
dowager asked her. 'Very well,' said my mother, who had
frequently visited the town. 'I hear he's had his gates mended,'
came back the reply.

Apart from people snobs there are, of course, the baby
snobs – who always refer to the au pair as nanny. 'It's so
vulgar to dress babies in anything else but little dresses,' said
one girl and went on to tell me about some friends of hers who
had adopted a baby. 'They've discovered the father was an Old
Etonian, they're awfully pleased about it.'

But best of all are the splendidly dotty aristocracy with their
endless nicknames: Piggy, Bunty, Dodo. But God, they can
curl you up.

We took one hoary old lady to the cinema and she insisted
on seeing *Guess Who's Coming to Dinner*. Having snored her way
through the second feature she surfaced at Sidney Poitier's
entrance, and yelled down the row in parade-ground tones:
'I hear that nigger's had his nose straightened.'

19 A Deadly Sin

The deadly sin I have the most trouble with is Gluttony. Every morning, on waking, I finger my rolls of superfluous flesh and vow that today will herald the dawn of a newer, slimmer Cooper.

It never works. Every evening, I go to bed a sadder and a wider woman, acutely conscious of having eaten too much, racked by fantasies about becoming the fat lady in a circus, or being doomed to an eternity of tastefully draped V-necked dresses from Evans the Outsize Shop.

The reasons for my predicament are threefold. First, I adore food; second, I am devoid of self-control; and third, the moment I feel bored, unhappy or frustrated, I start eating. The slightest setback: a cross word from my husband or one of the cats, an abusive letter from the Gas Board, a friend cutting me in the street, sends me post haste to the bread bin and the marmalade pot.

A quick rundown on my cronies gets the same answer. 'As soon as my lover went to Spain,' said one girl, 'I started gorging myself.' 'Greed comes over me like a terrible sexual compulsion whenever I feel low,' said another. 'I don't even taste what I'm eating, I just keep on. Every time my husband goes to pick up his children from his first wife I wolf a whole packet of biscuits.'

It seems a pity the manufacturers can't package self-control instead of those nasty slimming biscuits, which taste like cement between two pieces of blotting paper, or those revolting sweetening tablets that make a perfectly good cup of coffee undrinkable.

My husband, who lost over a stone when he gave up drinking for six weeks, believes it's alcohol that puts on the weight. But I think it's the fact that drink undermines one's good resolutions. Once I get a few gins and tonics inside me I think: To hell with slimming, men like a nice cosy armful anyway. Then I head straight for the salted almonds.

My more affluent friends cope with the slimming problem by having appetite-killing injections, living on meat and citrus fruits and, as a result, becoming terrible drags to have to dinner. Or else they steal off to Entrail Hall and return ten days later, irrigated at every orifice, thinner, paler and demonstrably smugger. I have toyed with the idea of joining them, but some miserly streak in my nature rebels against paying a fortune for ten days' starvation. Cheaper to buy a padlock for the fridge.

And all those different diets. You name it, I've tried it and haven't stuck to it. Slimming exercises are no good either because they make my husband howl with laughter. I've tried pasting photographs of girls in bikinis on all the biscuit tins, I have even hung a large mirror in the kitchen so that I can stare at myself every time I start eating. I look so disgusting it worked at first, but I'm now inured even to that.

It's quite impossible to slim in our house because no one sets me a good example. The cat is pregnant and is eating for at least a dozen. Time and again, I've cooked three courses for a dinner party the following night, and come into the kitchen to find my husband has scoffed the lot. And our lodger is just like the charwoman in the N. F. Simpson play who came in every day to finish up the leftovers: 'I've eaten the rice pudding and the fish pie, but I haven't been able to manage the steak and kidney pudding.'

And why is one so ashamed of being fat? – ripping out the size 14 label before showing off a new dress to the rest of the office – or, like a friend of mine, always explaining her plumpness to shop assistants by saying she hasn't got her figure back yet after the baby. Her children are ten and five.

And why are we so ashamed of gluttony? The number of bright conversations I've carried on desperately trying to conceal the fact that a chocolate biscuit is melting up my sleeve, or my cheeks are bulging with cold sprouts.

The fact is that nothing equals the bliss of losing weight, the sheer joy of being able to throw oneself down on somebody's lap without having to leave both feet on the ground to spread the load, or being lifted up by some playful admirer without his turning purple and the veins standing out on his forehead.

A friend of mine was so delighted to shed two stones that she went down to the butcher's and made him weigh out the equivalent in meat, so she could see what she had lost. 'It was wonderful,' she sighed afterwards. 'There were two legs of lamb, a small turkey, four pounds of liver and a mass of pork chops.'

Yet although I yearn to be *mince* myself, all the people I love most have large appetites, if not for food, then for drink or cigarettes or sex. And all my great loves in history or literature, Byron, Falstaff, Hamlet, Oscar Wilde and wicked old Henry VIII, seem also to have had a weight problem.

I admire self-control in others, but I'm far more seduced by self-indulgence. One of the things that endears my husband to me most is the way his lip trembles when he sees the last finger of whisky poured into someone else's glass.

But if you ever feel really low about being fat, turn to *Roget's Thesaurus*, and read what it says about being thin: 'THIN – spare, meagre, skinny, bony, cadaverous, fleshless, skin and bone, haggard, weedy, scrawny, lantern-jawed, hatchet-faced.'

Still want to slim?

20 Take Four Girls

Jilly Cooper imagines herself sharing a flat again:

We are four girls – we share a flat. We knot our headscarves under our chins like guardsmen, and every Friday morning we block the luggage compartment of the 30 bus, taking pigskin suitcases of dirty washing home to Mummy. On Sunday Mummy sends us back to London with clean washing, the pick of Daddy's herbaceous and a large fruit cake no one will ever eat.

We exist on scrambled eggs, cups of coffee and the hope that some day a prince will come and take us away from all this squalor. We share a bedroom like the dormitory at school. Clothes are piled to the ceiling on the one chair, the chest of drawers groans beneath a battalion of unstoppered jars and unwashed cups. Someone's blond wig languishes in a pool of spilt make-up.

The kitchen is decorated with peeling travel posters and un-washed milk bottles, and in the bathroom, talcum powder and dust lie deep and crisp and even on the pipes and the linoleum. The bath, ringed with high-water marks like a foot-ball sweater, is hidden beneath a dripping tropical jungle of stockings and bras.

In the evening, the drawing room is filled with girls with scarlet faces drying long mousy hair; or friends from other flats come to supper, balancing toasted cheese on their big knees. On the mantelpiece sit the fixtures: "Gideon, Rodney and Alastair at Home – bring a bottle'; a garden party; a few weddings. When we moved in, the landlord laid down lots of rules about not having men in, nor playing budgerigars after 10.30, but we don't take much notice. The gramophone blares Herb Alpert into the small hours.

We are four girls, we share a flat:

RACHEL is a receptionist who has been frogmarching her boy friend Gideon up and down in front of the Gas Board show-room for months in a desperate attempt to make him propose.

SAMANTHA puts 'model' on her passport, but usually works on stands at Olympia. This week she's at the Dairy Show, and the flat is filled with large men with mottled hands and straw in their turn-ups.

VIRGINIA is engaged, and smug to boot. Her 'fiasco' is abroad in some Huzzars or other, so she is in every night getting on our nerves and giving advice about our lovelife. 'Men only want one thing,' she claims – but appears to have forgotten what it is.

Virginia once tried to organize the housekeeping: 'You Scrub the floor this week, Samantha, then Rachel can do the shopping.' But we took no notice and she took umbrage and now buys her own All Bran and Peanut Butter, and writes Virginia on them in Magic Marker. One day Samantha came home early and crossed out all the 'ia's'.

Monday and chaos. Rachel is giving a little dinner party tomorrow to bring Gideon up to scratch. If anything makes Gideon scratch, says Samantha, it will be the sight of the grey-ing sheets on Rachel's bed. Rachel has also invited some newlyweds to encourage Gideon. She stays up half the night making a kipper *pâté* stiff with bones and borrowing rose-patterned plates from Terence and Jeremy upstairs. The rest of us have promised to go to the cinema.

On Tuesday, Rachel spends her lunch hour buying Yugoslav Riesling, candles, flowers, veal at 14s. a pound, and a long roll of French bread, which causes raised eyebrows in the Tube.

It is a short film and we all get back from the cinema to find Rachel in hysterics. The newlyweds are having a row; Gideon has only just arrived – drunk; the dinner burnt out hours ago, and Rachel has been slaving over a hot tin opener all evening to produce the kind of meal that Gideon will find it easy to do without for the rest of his life.

The trouble with life is that either Half London is after you jamming the wires for dates, or no one is, and you sit around eating chocolates, listening to Frank Sinatra and talking about getting a job abroad.

Wednesday, and a strange man is here for breakfast wearing Samantha's pink dressing gown, which doesn't quite look him. Samantha helps him to the last of Virginia's All Bran. 'He's used my toothbrush too,' hisses Virginia.

We are four girls, we share a hat—puke-green felt, which one of us wears if ever she has to go to a wedding. Rachel has one this afternoon – St Peter's, Eaton Square, and at least two bus loads of tenants.

Each time the telephone rings it's Virginia's mother ringing to discuss wedding plans. We wonder who will wear the communal hat to Virginia's wedding. At two in the morning, the doorbell rings. It must be Gideon, thinks Rachel. A proposal at last. Off with the rollers, on with Samantha's pink dressing gown. It's only three drunks from the Dairy Show wanting coffee and Samantha. But Samantha hasn't come home.

Next morning, Samantha's mother rings at breakfast also wanting Samantha. 'She's just popped out to buy the papers,' lies Virginia. Hastily she rings Samantha, who is curled happily round Gideon in Onslow Gardens, and tells her to ring her mother at once.

We are four girls, we share a flat. Samantha thinks she's pregnant. It must be one of those men from the Mechanical Handling Exhibition. Virginia said at the time their handling of Samantha was far from mechanical. Samantha is heavily overdrawn and the rent's not the only thing that's overdue.

Friday and Rachel is not speaking to Samantha. She is packing and putting instant tan on her face so that Mummy won't think she looks pale and ask questions about Gideon all week-end.

But it's payday. To hell with everything. To cheer herself up Rachel goes to Fenwicks and when she gets back to the flat everyone else has been to Fenwicks and bought the same. We are three girls, we share a flat. We look like the chorus from *White Horse Inn*.

21 Favourite Fantasies

Whenever life becomes too boring or unpleasant, I retreat into a world of make-believe, where my *alter ego* – who is at least a stone lighter than I am – carries on a vainglorious life quite unrelated to my real existence.

I am not too happy about this 'me' of my fantasies. I watch her sometimes, slinking out of the house at dawn clad only in a mink coat, her hair dyed some exotic colour, and roaring off to Hyde Park in her Ferrari where two American publishers are fighting a duel over her next book, then on to breakfast at the Connaught with the victor, followed by a morning's shopping at Asprey's, and lunch at the Ritz with Yves Montand. The afternoon I draw a veil over, but seven o'clock sees her off to the Bahamas for the week-end with eight pig-skin suitcases.

Fantasizing began when I was a child. I used to daydream continually about rescuing my nanny and my teddy-bear from a blazing house, while I myself perished in the flames and everyone, including a slightly singed bear, sobbed themselves silly at my funeral.

As I grew older, I imagined myself performing similar feats of daring but now dressed as a boy. In turn I was Dick Barton, D'Artagnan and for at least a year Nelson's cabin-boy defeating the French fleet single-handed – my sex only being discovered when a cannon-ball shattered my thigh, whereupon Nelson would exclaim: 'Gad sir, it's a gel, and a demned brave one at that,' as I lay dying in his arms.

Later I switched to horses. Every car or train journey was whiled away jumping walls, hedges and houses as they flashed by. I read *National Velvet* and *The Maltese Cat*, and dreamed of winning the National and polo matches with a broken collarbone. Then I went away to school, and my favourite fantasy became riding home from a show, my pony garlanded with red rosettes like Poppy Day, and suddenly finding my form-mistress sitting in a puddle with a broken ankle. I would heave her on to my pony and bear her home to tea, whereupon she would clasp me warmly by the hand and say gruffly: 'You're not such a clot after all.'

I was also preoccupied with being famous. Not being a great washer, I thought about becoming a Rank starlet, and every time I thumped out the 'Merry Peasant' I saw myself as Eileen Joyce, playing Grieg at the Albert Hall, changing my dress between movements. I would glide on to the platform to clamorous applause – white shoulders gleaming out of clouds of net, a cigarette holder in one hand, and in the other a long umbrella, which to me in those days epitomized chic.

When I was twelve I started dreaming about men. I became a wanton, tempestuous beauty tamed and reduced to swooning submission by one gangster after another. Members of the Mafia, Henri of Guise, a long scar running down his handsome face, Slim Callaghan, Kirk Douglas in an eyepatch, sundry Goths and Visigoths; all took turns to knock me into shape.

Even allowing for poetic licentiousness, I am not proud of my fantasy self – I never dreamed of a life serving others, of being a nurse or a nun in the Congo, and I quite ruthlessly exterminated my dear parents. Heroines in fantasies never have parents – they are defenceless orphans or, in my case, alone and palely loitering with intent.

About the age of fourteen I discovered Georgette Heyer and tennis players. I went to Wimbledon for the first time, and those bronzed, beautiful, stupid men affected me like a fever. I now saw myself as the laughing rebellious ward of a US tennis champion called Sexias, who had chinky eyes and a reputation for bad temper. Gardner Mulloy, Budge Patty and Frank Sedgeman were all fighting for my hand, but I only cared for my wicked guardian, who in turn only realized he couldn't live without me when I fainted after winning the Singles, Doubles *and* the Plate.

All these fantasies were very innocent. My heroes raised quizzical eyebrows but never anything else. They would kiss me passionately, as rockets exploded in my head. Then a row of asterisks would follow until Stage Two; when, tears streaming down his face, Kirk Douglas or the Duc de Guise would be holding my hands, as I smiled weakly up at him after producing the heir he had so long desired.

Eventually I left school, and real men took over – after my dream heroes, they were a bit of an anti-climax, particularly the first time I was kissed. No rockets, no stars, not even asterisks. The odd thing too is that in real life the men I like are merry, sensitive, sensual extroverts, quite unlike the haughty, cruel, humourless introverts of my dreams.

I don't think men fantasize nearly as much as women. My husband says he occasionally dreams of making a hundred before lunch for Yorkshire at Headingley, or the stands rising at Twickenham when he scores the vital try. When he was younger he imagined himself driving off in a sports car with a lush blonde, saying: ''Bye, Ted, 'Bye, Christopher, 'Bye, Paul, see you!' to his admiring friends.

People are always telling me I ought to daydream less and face up to the real world. But unless fantasies are used as a complete substitute for action, I can't see much harm in them. We all need the pipe dream of writing the great novel, or winning the pools, or becoming managing director and kicking all our colleagues in the teeth. The world is deep and dark and full of tigers, and we need those shimmering white castles in the air to creep into when life gets unbearable.

As Donne says: 'If I dream I have you, I have you.'

But frankly I don't need to fantasize much these days, I lead such a full life. I've just finished washing up a tea party for all my son's little friends from Buckingham Palace, and putting the next month's meals in the deep freeze. Anthony Powell and Angus Wilson will be popping in for drinks soon to read me advance proofs of their rave reviews of my first novel, and later the Rolling Stones, Geoff Boycott, Goldie Hawn, Iris Murdoch, Giullini, Mary Whitehouse, Ken Russell, Mr

Ryland, Mr Jackson, nice Lord Hall and Robert Graves will be joining us for an intimate little dinner. Robert's staying on a few days – he won't stop anywhere else when he's in London.

Yves is right – this dress with horizontal stripes does *suit* me; goodness, I really must take the home-made bread out of the oven. I wonder who's sent me four dozen red roses?

22 Dirty Tricks

Out to dinner the other evening, an extremely fast piece started reading palms. First she captivated my husband by fondling his fingers and telling him he had the hands of a true lover, then she put me down by saying my hands indicated 'small-mindedness, calculation and a surprising lack of sexual drive.'

Everyone laughed a great deal, and this set me brooding on the whole art of social warfare, undermining one's fellows by mean little tricks like turning your bathroom scales up three-quarters of a stone when an enemy's coming to dinner, or arriving very early for dinner at someone else's house, and rampaging with their children until they get so over-excited they won't go to sleep.

As a guest you can also have fun killing a party stone dead by asking if you can turn on the television to watch a half-hour programme on refugees. Or, if it's a children's party, you have only to scratch your head reflectively and tell the other Mums how all the boys at Dominic's school have got nits. Or, if it's a private view of an art gallery, you can hang your maxi coat over your enemy's most 'meaningful' piece of sculpture.

Another sneaky guest trick – when a girl has asked you in for a drink with only *one* other couple, you ring up her best friend the morning after and say: 'Samantha's party was fun, I was surprised she hadn't invited you.'

There are tricks too for the male guest. If you only want to get drunk at a dance and not take your share of dancing with the wallflowers, a bandage round the ankle works wonders. Equally, at a cocktail party, if you don't want to be cajoled into taking some girl out to dinner, always wear a dinner jacket, then people assume you're either a waiter or going on somewhere.

Being a hostess gives you massive scope for mean tricks: 'Could you possibly give Samantha a lift down from London,' you say. 'Oh, how kind, she's bringing the family, and it would have been such hell for her to take three children under three on a 200-mile train journey.'

Or: 'We're thinking of having a few people in for drinks . . . what are you doing on Saturday? Nothing! Oh good, then you won't mind doing the rugger teas for me, then I can devote all afternoon getting ready for my party.'

Or (if it's some dollybird your husband lusts after): 'Wear your warmest dress, the central heating has broken down.' Then, by the time she arrives, the central heating has made a miraculous recovery and is turned up to tropical, so she spends the whole evening pouring with sweat and is puce in the face.

Another ruse – when you don't want to have people back, but your conscience is pricking – is to ask them at the last moment, when they won't have time to arrange a baby-sitter, or at Christmas and Easter, when they're bound to be away. On the same principle, hand out invitations to a vast party in August, when everyone's on holiday.

You can also have fun giving false identities – telling a gold-digger that the shaggy layabout in the corner is really a millionaire, or a snob that the most boring man at the party is a marquis, or a swelled-headed sexual athlete that the local lesbian is madly in love with him.

From the woman's point of view, if there's a beautiful rival staying in the same house in summer, you can ensure her being covered in bites (insect rather than male) by nipping upstairs during the evening, on the pretext of turning down beds, and switching her light on, and opening her window.

Or, if she's after the son of the house, you can discredit her with the hostess by slipping a few empty gin bottles under the bed when she's not looking.

Women are so skilled in bitching each other up, that scoring off them can be tricky, but next time an enemy shows you some new photographs, pick out the one with buck teeth, the squint and the ostrich feet round the eyes and say: 'Now that one really *is* like you.'

There's also the art of making other people feel mean. Wait until they've run someone down for twenty minutes before saying: 'How odd, she's my favourite sister,' or let an anti-Semitic diatribe run its full course before you casually tell the assembled company you're three-quarters Jewish.

Present giving also has possibilities, a random selection being: sweaters with horizontal stripes for fat girls; loud cacophonous musical instruments for children whose parents you don't like; oil paints for children whose ditto parents have just had their house re-decorated; huge boxes of chocolates for anyone on a diet; a female kitten, when you've sworn it's a Tom, for practically anyone.

Most people will be able to supply their own mean tricks, whether it's one-way mirrors or changing signposts.

My favourites are: throwing someone a bag of walnuts and saying: 'Eggs! Catch!'; taking someone wearing a wig for a drive on a motorway, and suggesting you put the hood down; or suggesting to the man in the dark blue suit, that he goes in the back seat with Lassie who's moulting.

But most profitable of all is offering someone a lift in your taxi, and hopping out just before they reach their destination, saying: 'You can get this on expenses, can't you?'

23 Old Girls' Mags

Confined to bed with 'flu this week, I have been studying a number of girls' school magazines. Incredible though it may seem, the following extracts are taken verbatim from the Old Girls' Notes. They recall all the jolly hockeysticking rumbustiousness of school life, as one arrested Sixthformer after another takes up her pen.

Mary Sopwith (née Snatch) writes: 'Life is very hectic at the moment with John (three), Samantha (one), Henry and Archie (six months) and the parrot (twelve), but we are now safely ensconced in our olde worlde cottage on Windermere and I am still finding time for my W.I. activities. Maureen Ramm (née Binns) blew in last week in her Mini, and, quite by chance, Louise Plunkett sailed across the lake in time for tea, so the tongues were really wagging! Louise reports that her sister Jennifer is currently working her way round Australia as cook, cleaner and partial deckhand on a prawnboat.'

But if the pace of daily life is fast and furious, all hell breaks loose when our Old Girls go on holiday: Angela Fish, going to pieces in the grand manner, writes: 'I had a most memorable month in Tunisia. Friends at school will remember my passion for camels.' Mollie Parker has just had another son who 'took her by surprise while they were on holiday in Eire', while Florence Graham grumbles: 'I have just returned from my beloved Rome but found it quite spoilt. So many foreigners live there, and also Italians.'

Jean Ellis, however, enjoyed her honeymoon in Holland, where she saw 'much of interest'. Alas, the Notes reveal, her sister Phyllis fared less well in Cyprus: 'It was far too hot, especially as Phyllis was having Tarquin, who arrived on August 8th.'

Even the punctuation seems to have gone to the dogs on Sarah Thrust-Pointer's holiday: 'My husband Margaret aged three and I have just returned from a hectic fortnight camping in France.'

The sporting side isn't neglected either. Alice Turner writes: 'Mother is still finding time to play cricket for Berkhamsted, and whenever I get a free Saturday I join Joyce Evans in a game of Lax for Liverpool Ladies.'

For those not so keen on good clean fun, there appears to be a great deal of rough-housing: 'I ran into Dorothy Beard last week, and I am constantly bumping into Gladys Grimmet, who broke her femur last year, made a marvellous recovery, and then fractured the other one.' Why on earth don't they look where they're going?

Yet amid this violence, Old Girls still have time for hobbies – fly fishing on the Dee for instance: 'I take the beat opposite Balmoral,' writes Elizabeth Beresford Cripps. "One day the Queen Mother came down with her corgis running around her, and I wondered how to perform a suitable bob in breast waders standing knee deep in water. But she spotted us, and with her charming smile turned further up the river.'

School mistresses, too, still receive veneration: 'It was a pleasant surprise to find Miss Horsfall living in Rye,' writes Angela Peel. And when younger Old Girls move to other schools they are deeply shocked by the laxity of behaviour.

'The climax of my first day at school,' writes Anthea Broad plaintively, 'was when I set off on a cross-country run. As it was the first day, I had not brought any games clothes – but nor had anyone else, so I wasn't worried. I was appalled, however, when everyone started off on the run without a games skirt. Imagine running through the streets of Wolverhampton in flimsy navy knickers!' No doubt the Wolves enjoyed it.

There are also some sad little entries: 'Jennifer and Sally Good say they have nothing to report.' No news is Good news presumably. And there is poor Janet Higgins, 'who was having a very gay time in London, but is now living in the wilds of Scotland for nine months'.

Judith Pratt writes: 'Apart from getting married, I have no news except that I have taken up fencing. Most of my husband's friends seem to be married to Old Girls.' A contribution which leaves one feeling quite helpless.

When I was at school, one of the main stumbling blocks was that one was only allowed to consort with about a dozen girls in the entire school – all of one's own age. If one made friends with older girls one was accused of soliciting, if one approached younger girls it was open proof of an aberrant libido.

But on becoming an Old Girl, it's a glorious free-for-all. Irrespective of age, one can become bosom friends with any one of the Jumbo Jet Set, from the ex-secretary of the rambling club to the school bully. There is no flat-chested crone waiting to spy on you, or accuse you of sexual promiscuity, as you whizz off in your mini wearing navy-blue knickers, bump into Alice Clark, have a breathless chinwag with old Sally what's it, struggle into breast waders, and rush off for a quick game of Lax with Miss Horsfall, now surprisingly enough living in Horsham.

Oh, the speed and delight of being an Old Girl, even if one is ninety-six and can only just manage to weed the garden from one's wheelchair! For nearly every entry in these magazines expressed the earnest wish that 'any Old Girl passing through or living in the area would call in for coffee and a chat'.

My favourite contribution on these lines came from Geraldine Gibson Bullock, who 'is doing research up the Amazon and hopes any Old Girls in the area will drop in'. I only hope she won't be inundated by hordes of monkeys wearing felt hats and gym slips.

24 Telephonitis

I loathe the telephone – vile shrill-voiced intruder. I'd never answer it at all if I didn't feel I might be missing something: a million-pound offer from a film company or Robert Mitchum asking me out to lunch. I hate the element of uncertainty – you never know if it's going to be a friend or a foe on the line. I wish they'd invent a telephone which turned green like the breath-test bag when it was an enemy ringing, so I needn't answer it.

I hate the way it always rings when I'm washing my hair, or putting on instant tan so when I've rung off I never know which bits of me I've tanned, and I end up striped like an okapi.

I hate the way I'm incapable of finishing a conversation and I always end up saying let's have lunch or come and have a drink to people when I don't want to see them at all.

I hate the way the telephone intrudes on our lives. At 5.30 the other morning it roused me from heavy slumber. Thinking someone must be dead, I snatched up the receiver but all I could hear was two bass voices very discordantly singing 'In the Autumn of Our Lives', followed by cackles of Bourbon-soaked laughter.

It was my husband and a chum in New York, ringing up for a chat. They had forgotten about the time-lag.

Usually when the telephone murders sleep, it's the team secretary of some cricket club ringing: 'We've got a slightly hysterical problem about the Stragglers of Asia,' they say. 'Can you think of eight people who could play on Sunday?'

Then there was the hideous occasion when my husband's

boss rang up at 8.30, and I mistook him for the Rugger captain. 'You are an old pig waking us so early,' I said. 'Hang on while I draw the curtains, I haven't got a stitch on.'

I then proceeded to tell him that my husband could not play Rugger that afternoon. He was working for incompetent amateurs during the week and he didn't want to play for more incompetent amateurs at the week-end.

Ideally, I suppose one should have a secretary to keep telephoners at bay. My previous char did her best: 'Mrs Cooper's residence,' she would say in refained tones and when I got back from shopping there would be a string of messages:

'A gentleman phoned – *very urgent* – could you call him at once? A lady – *I think* – rang, would you ring her this afternoon?' Which did not leave me much wiser.

Or like a friend of mine who went out, leaving her new au pair in the house, and rang in later to ask her to put on the joint. 'Hello, Francesca,' she said. 'It's Mrs Scott here.'

'Mrs Scott no here, back 5.30,' said Francesca firmly.

'No, this is Mrs Scott herself speaking.'

'Mrs Scott no here – back 5.30.'

Nothing could evoke a different response – it was like trying to make the Speaking Clock lady suddenly launch into Eskimo Nell.

I also resent the passing of the old exchanges. Gone is the romance of Fox Lane and Gipsy Hill, gone the kudos of a Belgravia telephone number – 235 isn't the same thing at all.

A man I know claims that the test of a good party is to wake up next morning and find your cigarette packet covered in telephone numbers.

But the fun's gone out of that now. In the good old days you could distinguish the HAMpstead Bohemians from the FLAxman hippies or the twin-set-and-pearl brigade in KENsington. But not any more. Now you ring up a girl, ask her out and only discover when you've looked in the *A to Z Guide* that you've got to trail all the way out to THOrnton Heath.

There are compensations: it's wonderful the way you can now dial the Continent, get straight through to your lover in WORms or BERgen Op Zoom, say 'Hello darling, I love you,' and ring off, and it might only cost you 2p.

Of course, some people adore the telephone, curling up on the carpet, cradling it like a favourite cat in their laps, or wandering round the house plugging it into the hot cupboard, the dog kennel or wherever they may be. One friend is such a compulsive telephoner that he can't pass a call box without going in and ringing someone; but then he can't let an empty taxi pass without flagging it down to make up for all the times he can't get one.

And the telephone has its advantages. I know a newly married couple who are so besotted with each other that they have an early call put in each morning so that they can make love before going to work.

Best of all I love crossed lines. I listen to them for hours. A friend of mine said he stumbled on two vets talking about putting down cows. He terrified the life out of them by mooing into the telephone.

My grandfather once had a memorable crossed line in Yorkshire.

'Hast thou a Manx cat?'

'Nay, but I can make thee one.'

25 Shopping

My housekeeping bills are astronomical. I can't understand those women who manage to feed a family of six on £6 a week. 'Oh, Gideon loves herrings in oatmeal and tripe and onions,' they cry smugly. 'But, of course, I only shop once a week, I take the car down to the market and load everything in.'

I, on the other hand, shop every day, often twice. How do I know on Friday what I or the cats will want to eat on Monday, and what happens if we suddenly get popular and are asked out five nights running? All those leeks and cabbages will go rotten.

Besides, I find that bulk shopping never does anything but increase our bulk. Rows of tins in the larder just encourage midnight feasts. And I always get rooked in the market, those hard little tomatoes piled neatly at the front of the stall bear no relation to the red squashed purée that has soaked through the paper bag when I get home.

I'm a sucker for supermarkets, though, everything from walnut whips to Sunny Jim Firelighters, and I always fall for tinned food when it says: '3s. 9d. our price', then I go round the corner and find the same tins selling at their normal price of 3s. But I enjoy shopping every day: catching up on local gossip, reading the latest exploits of Biffo the Bear and Lord Snooty in the launderette, and the betting shop is just like a cocktail party, you see half Fulham there.

Shopping with a baby, of course, has distinct advantages. We could live for days on the loot my son manages to inveigle out of the local shopkeepers: slab chocolate, lollipops, slices of liver sausage and sherbet from the off-licence.

86

There are disadvantages, too. I've never dared tell the man at the dry cleaners he's got my son's sex wrong. 'Isn't she a darling little girl' he says, every time we go past. 'Isn't she growing.' The 'darling little girl' is also inclined to run amok in the baker's and start cramming éclairs into and all over his face, and he's developed a disreputable habit of goosing fat ladies in front of him, when he doesn't think a queue is moving fast enough.

I hate queuing, too. I can feel my blood pressure rocketing as the woman in front of me wants to know how many baked beans there are in every tin, or at the bank when I get behind someone who is paying in six months' takings and I have to hang about reading leaflets on deposit accounts while mountains of sixpences are shovelled back and forth.

Because I'm a compulsive clothes buyer, the local dress shops are not quite my line of country. At Reena's they sell OS vests and salmon-pink directoire knickers big enough for a hippopotamus, and at Madame Doris, which caters for a better class of customer, you can buy open-weave green knit-wear and Cross Your Heart stretch bras on the HP.

Of course, buying clothes anywhere is a hazardous oper-ation. There's those terrible moustachioed crones who dart out of shops in Oxford Street and draw you in with red-nailed claws, if you so much as glance in the windows. Once inside you're doomed. They hustle you into a changing room and some hideous dress, and seem to have the answer to every complaint. If you hate the dress's colour, they tell you 'it's being worn a lot this year'. If it's too tight, they maintain the material stretches; if too loose, you must allow for shrinkage.

So, in despair, you complain it doesn't fit. 'Our fitter can fix that in a trice,' they say, and rustle up some top-heavy frump dripping pins like Moby Dick, who's started taking darts before you can explain you don't want the dress anyway.

But although they're hoping for you to buy something, the fuss they make if you try to pay by cheque – the cards of identity they require, the fingerprints and the photographs they insist on taking (I always irritate them by asking if I can have a print). Sometimes they even warn you that closed circuit tele-vision is watching you. This appeals to my exhibitionist tendencies, I get insane urges to thrust ten pairs of Da-Glo green knickers into my bag, shouting 'Can you see me, mother' into the camera.

Whenever I go to big department stores, there seems to be a Whites Sale on, or it's Flying Duck Week, or Suspender Belt Event; and those big mirrors everywhere disconcert me a bit. Being nearsighted I'm always charging up to my own reflection and asking it the way to the lifts. However, the Ladies are useful as changing rooms for M & S next door.

I love watching women go home in the bus after shopping. Disillusion usually sets in about Shepherd's Bush. They can't resist opening those complicated box carrier-bags, which you can never do up again, and peering in at their new dress so subtly cyclamen in the shop, but now emerging as a far too shocking pink. One woman I know deserves a degree in shopping, M.A. Oxon. Street. She comes up to Oxford Street from the country three times a week, the first jaunt to buy, the second jaunt to take back what she'd bought and the third to reconnoitre for next week.

Shoe buying, too, is a drag, for some reason they only bring single shoes, so you hobble round in one bunion crusher, trying to assess the effect in a looking glass only a foot high. 'Oh, you'll wear them in,' they say brightly when you complain they're uncomfortable. But not before they wear you out.

Shoe shopping in Italy is evidently different. A beautiful, heavily pregnant friend of mine was buying boots in Rome when suddenly the black-eyed dago serving her clamped a warm hand on her bottom. 'You haf the bluest, bluest eyes I haf every seen,' he said. Ah, the Dolcis Vita.

26 Me and Non-me

Fifteen years ago, Professor Ross set the middle classes by the ears by introducing U and Non-U. Now the arrival of kitsch has got them on the hop again, creeping out at the dead of night to bury their garden gnomes and Pope John ashtrays. So this time I'm going to have my bitsch and offer another set of standards – Me and Non-Me.

U-people, for example, were never supposed to run. Me-people run all the time because they're late, or it's raining and they've lost their umbrellas. They also run upstairs and up bills.

Me-people are besotted about animals – cats, horses, dogs. But not to the nauseating extent of putting diamanté collars round their necks or clipping ruffs and peacocks on poodles' coats. Budgerigars and canaries are Non-Me. Goldfish are not only Non-Me but also rather an expensive way of feeding one's cat.

Parrots are very Me because you can have fun teaching them Non-Me expressions like 'Sit ye down' and 'Cheerio', which enrage the Me-people that own them. Other Non-Me expressions include: 'Good morning to you', 'Take a pew', 'Don't stand on ceremony', 'What's your poison?' and 'How are the folks at home?'

People referring to 'Your good lady', 'Your better half', 'Your lady wife' or 'Your hubby' are also Non-Me. Me-people call their wives 'Darling'. Non-Me people call them 'Dear'. Non-Me couples call each other 'Mummy' and 'Daddy'.

Net curtains are Non-Me, because sunshine is Me. Orange net lavatory seat covers topped by a yellow rose are Non-Me,

89

particularly when they come with dolls in orange net dresses to cover the spare roll of loo paper.

It's also Non-Me to carry your clothes round in quilted plastic containers, or to hang them on mauve silk padded coathangers, or even worse on coathangers of Tony Blackburn's head and shoulders.

Non-Me people refer to their cars as 'she' and furnish them with rubber lolling doggies and swivelling birds. Purely functional things in cars like refrigerators, television and cocktail cabinets are very Me.

Non-Me babies are smothered in lemon swansdown. Non-Me little girls wear jewellery, particularly tiny gold ear-rings, and carry plastic white bags with pink plastic looking-glasses inside. Non-Me little boys wear bow ties and buster suits and have their hair cut too short.

Non-Me people are tediously preoccupied with good wines. Me-people think quantity is far more important than quality.

Non-Me people put their initials on everything – signet rings, shirts, cigarette lighters and particularly on petitions to bring back hanging.

Me-people get pregnant. Non-Me people expect happy events or little strangers. Non-Me people never 'die', they simply 'pass away'. Non-Me animals never 'die', they go to 'the happy hunting ground'.

Short-sleeved shirts for men with little nicks in the sleeves are Non-Me. So are zodiac ties, belted camel-hair coats, slot-in pre-folded handkerchiefs and fill-in polo necks. Non-Me women wear trousers with straps under the ankle, plastic pixie hoods and transparent galoshes.

Me-women wear as few underclothes as possible. Non-me women wear bras, petticoats and vests under see-through blouses so all you can see is rigging.

Christmas cards to 'You and yours' with 'hearty and sincere good wishes' are Non-Me. So are people who have their cards printed with their children's photographs on.

Non-Me people give names like The Nookery to numbered houses, and put them on their writing paper in Gothic script. They also start their letters 'Just a Line', keep on saying 'Well,

Jill' throughout, and end up: 'I must close now, yours truly Samantha Cavendish (near Miss).'

Non-Me people call you by your Christian name every two minutes, or even worse by someone else's Christian name.

Me-people are non-militant, never get 'disgusted' except by violence or cruelty. 'Angry housewives', 'Irate mothers of five', 'Outraged councillors', who are always belly-aching on television, are Non-Me. So are feminists rabbiting on about woman's place being neither in the home nor on her back.

Students terrify the life out of me, and are therefore Non-Me. Once they become graduates, they're Me again.

Bagpipes are Non-Me. So are string quartets, madrigals and unaccompanied voices. Me-composers are Wagner, Verdi, Brahms and Mahler, Me-writers are St Simon, Jane Austen, Proust and Anthony Powell.

Tonic is Me; bitter lemon is Non-Me.

Me-people show blue movies; Non-Me people show slides. Me-people have 'big helpings'; Non-Me people take 'generous portions'. Me-people sweat and have scurf; Non-Me people perspire and have dandruff. Me-people get dirty; Non-Me people get soiled.

Me-people have photographs of *other* people's wives on their desks, never use the word 'meaningful' or send out party invitations covered with cocks or cocktail glasses.

Non-Me men whip the Gold Spot out of their glove compartment and give their mouths a quick spray before pouncing on you. Non-Me women (and men for that matter) wear matching dresses and coats.

Me-people would never take an article like this seriously.

27 *Embarrassing Moments*

Are you squirming uncomfortably – then I'll begin. My most humiliating experience occurred when I was seven – the day my first pony arrived. Having boasted about it for weeks, I dragged several classmates home to witness the touching first meeting. They hung over the gate as I rushed up to this adorable, fluffy animal and flung my arms round its neck. Whereupon it turned round and bit me viciously. The derisive giggling of my friends echoes in my ears to this day.

But generally as a child, I found dogs more blush-making than ponies: big dogs that sniffed, small dogs that mounted one's leg at polite tea parties, and our own retriever who invariably mistook other people's pale-silk sofas for a lamppost.

Many children are crippled with embarrassment by parents wearing the wrong clothes at speech day. Mine were blameless in this respect, but my father did make me curl up by singing the bass part in church. I was convinced everyone must be staring at the little girl who was standing next to the big man singing the wrong tune.

Being lousy at games, or even worse, gym was also a constant source of humiliation. Thundering the length of the gymnasium with the whole class smirking and knowing you hadn't a hope of clearing that loathsome box; or the misery of team games, when two girls would pick sides and you were the last person left so you had to slink to one side unchosen.

Being in love too is fraught with embarrassment. I blush to remember how one of my great loves told my best friend (who promptly told me) that I kissed like a vacuum cleaner.

It put me off men for years. But I still giggle over the discomfort of the man who tried to pick me up in the Tube one morning and was appalled to find me sitting next to him at a dinner party that evening when he turned up with his intensely imposing wife.

My husband doesn't embarrass me very often, although twice at respectable parties he's sat on antique occasional tables and shattered them like match-wood. And when he's tight he's inclined to lie on his back and pretend he's a bear, although he usually confines this to the privacy of his own home.

I know I embarrass my husband by making too much noise when I get over-excited, by reading in the street and bumping into lamp-posts and by always looking immediately, whenever he says 'Don't look now, but . . .'

Being caught in the wrong of course is always embarrassing. A letter came for my husband the other morning from a very rich relation. Not being able to contain myself, I opened and read it, noted with relief and delight it contained a fat cheque and carefully sealed it up again. Later, my husband came home and went through his mail. 'Maggie must be going senile,' I heard him say irritably. 'She says she's sent me a cheque but she's forgotten to put it in.'

I froze with horror to see the cheque lying on the kitchen table; in my haste to seal up the letter I'd forgotten to put it back.

But my favourite caught-in-the-act story comes from a producer I know who was driving through Hollywood one arctic night when he saw a naked man loping along the street and flagging him down for a lift.

'What on earth happened to you?' asked my friend.

'Oh,' said the naked man, 'the husband came back.'

Another thing I find embarrassing is when people ring up at half an hour's notice and want to come and stay, and the sheets are all in the laundry basket and the towels – because we haven't bought any new ones since we were married – are all in holes and the texture of Brillo pads.

I am also embarrassed staying in other people's houses if they don't put locks on the loo door. Or at parties when you turn up in scruff order and everyone else is done up to the tens. Or when you faint from the heat and everyone assumes you're pregnant or drunk or both. Or when large females come up and ask you to dance. Or when other large females with huge busts suddenly whip one out and start feeding their offspring.

I also hate being made a fool of in public. I never know what to do with my face when men in Tyrolean dress come and sing at me in nightclubs; or at the pantomine when Dick Whitington's cat comes padding purposefully down the aisle and drags me on to the stage to be sawn in half or wave handkerchiefs.

My mother tells me that her most embarrassing moment was when she screwed herself up to have a blazing row with my brother's housemaster and, having routed him on every count, she swept out of his study. It was only when she was halfway down the stairs she discovered she'd left her knitting ball behind and had to follow the trail of wool all the way back to his study to collect it.

Finally: to cap all embarrassment stories, a friend of mine was in London for the day and suddenly saw a woman sitting opposite her in the Tube wearing exactly the same hat – red felt with a blue band. She started giggling at the woman and pointing at her own hat. The woman looked very tight-lipped and moved down the carriage, so my friend grinned round at everyone else and kept pointing at her hat.

No one grinned back. Most of them stared fixedly out of the window. Several got out at the next stop. It was only when she got out several stations later, and caught a glimpse of herself in a shop window that my friend realized what was the matter. In her haste to leave home she had put on her green beret instead of her red hat with the blue band.

28 Meanness

I loathe meanness. I am uncharmed by people who give me a present that has already been given to them by somebody else, or who bang on and on about paying for dinner, but never actually manage to produce their cheque books.

I dislike women who won't hold the loo door open for me because they don't see why I shouldn't pay my penny too, or who serve up prawn cocktails which are seven-eighths shredded lettuce, or who say: 'I'm dying to read your new book, I can't wait to get it out of the library.'

Mean people suck sweets surreptitiously, bulging out the cheek away from you, so they won't have to offer you one. They charge hitch-hikers for petrol, and when they've run over a rabbit they scrape it off the road for dinner.

Mean people plough their way through disgusting set meals, merely because they've paid for them. They dry out tea bags and use them again, and when they're given free theatre tickets, they flog them at the full price.

Someone the other week defined meanness as an obscene telephone caller who reverses the charges. My favourite niggard in the woodpile, however, was the man who when George V died, instead of buying a black tie, just inked out the stripes of his Old Etonian one. When the period of court mourning was over, he simply washed it.

Meanness is a great sexual turn-off. How can you get hung up on a man who invites you to the cinema, then suggests you meet in the bar, so you have to buy your own ticket to get in?

Afterwards, he makes you walk half an hour in a deluge to

a little place 'just round the corner', where he will briskly steer you away from the caviare towards the fresh grapefruit ('they chill it so well here'), and finally when the bill comes for £1.99 he will have the temerity to put down a quid and ask you if you have any change.

People are so hypocritical about their stinginess. 'It's awfully bourgeois to get married,' they say (when they are not getting hooked for tax returns). Or: 'I only do my accounts every week because it's so fascinating to see where the money goes.' (When they're bellyaching over an extra lollipop for the parrot.)

Beware too of spending week-ends with the stingy. You may take them a bottle of whisky but you will never see it again. At sundown every evening, your host will go out and water the gin. And your hostess will follow you round turning off lights and fires, and wincing each time you give the washing-up water an overdose of Quix or spread the butter so she can't see the toast underneath.

These people place a piggybank beside the telephone, and if cut off on the phone, they always wait for *you* to ring them back. I have a very rich girlfriend who invariably rings up and after a few seconds says: 'This is a frightful line, ring me back at 00000000' or some such number, and it's only after you've rung her and been gassing for half an hour, you discover she's ringing from the Grand Hotel, Honolulu.

The meanness of rich people, of course, never ceases to amaze. But as Adam Smith points out in *The Money Game*, no one ever has enough money. When you just make your pile, you go round flaunting your 'I'm a millionaire' badge, but then you realize there are an awful lot of people about wearing 'I'm a billionaire' badges, and you want one of those too, and so it goes on.

I suppose this explains Paul Getty's telephone box, and why one millionaire I met would not turn on his central heating until the icicles were hanging from the Gauguins. Another drives round Knightsbridge for hours when he's shopping looking for a meter with time on it, and yet another misses tube after tube in the morning rootling round in the litter bins for a discarded newspaper.

I know only one millionaire who is really generous – he has pockets stuffed with tenners, and hands out prom tickets as though he were dealing a bridge hand, but even he has funny values. He rang me the other day: 'Darling, darling, I've just bought two priceless first editions.'

'What are they?' I said.

'Don't know, I'll go and look.'

They were *Endymion* and Shelley's early poems.

It always intrigues me how mean people become when they're getting divorced – dividing up the notes of the chiming doorbell, haggling over who gets the breast or the wing of the flying duck. And it only takes the death of a rich relation to have the most loving family at each other's throats over the spoils.

Of course I can be very mean myself. I hate spending money on people I don't like, and I'm not wild about lending things: favourite books and clothes and particularly my husband – people are so awfully bad about giving him back.

But I think one of the reasons I avoid people who are parsimonious is because they make me feel guilty. I know I ought to be better with money, I never fill in my counterfoil, or know to the nearest £200 what horrors my bank statement has in store for me. . . .

Occasionally when I read Mrs Beeton or meet some man at a party who tells me what a marvellous little manager his wife is, I make feeble attempts to be more economical – serving up wafer-thin mince for dinner and keeping whites of eggs in the fridge for days in the forlorn hope that I might learn to make meringues.

If only I could save money by refingering gloves, or darning socks, or even mending torn sheets. You really do feel a failure as a 'little manager' if the only thing you can sew with any proficiency is wild oats.

But I was comforted to hear of an old lady who sounds even vaguer than I am. At the age of seventy-five, she suddenly thought she ought to start taking an interest in her bank statements.

'It's wonderful,' she said after a few months. 'The more money I spend, the more I have. The only thing I don't quite understand is why the bank has run out of black ink.'

29 *The Horrors of Heartiness*

Trailing back after a stay in the school sanatorium, I accidentally dropped a pair of knickers in the middle of Pitch 1. Later they were discovered by one of the gardeners who discreetly hung them on a goal post.

The incident caused unbridled mirth among my mates in the Upper Fourth, but was regarded as an act of dangerous iconoclasm by the games mistress who carpeted me and wrote on my end of term report:

'Jill doesn't take games seriously, she seems to lack any form of team spirit.'

She had my measure, of course. I was lousy at games, but I tried hard because I realized the best way to gain instant popularity was through glory on the playing fields. What I couldn't stomach was the dreadful heartiness of the whole caper. I was unmoved by the serge and thunder of the hockey team : vast girls with purple thighs and huge jacked-up busts heaving beneath their Aertex shirts, I hated cheering on the touchline, and bellowing 'Forty Years On' afterwards if we won the match. I found it more amusing to play up the games mistress than play the game. I received endless pep talks about letting the side down. I was never made a prefect.

Today I no longer take any exercise except Egyptian PT,* but I am still assaulted by guilt on cold winter afternoons. I feel I should be taking a brisk walk instead of curling up with a good bookie and the racing on television.

I cannot understand the mania for keeping fit – men in bowler hats cycling to work, executives brandishing their squash rackets. Fit for what, anyway ? Taking more exercise I

* Sleeping.

suppose, and getting lots of boring muscle which will turn to fat the moment they let up. I have never been fit in my life, I even pant when I run up a bill.

Nor can I understand the mania for getting outdoors. Take the looniness of the long distance runner – pounding along country lanes, so anxious to lop off seconds he never stops to marvel at a field of buttercups or a flock of geese against the sky. Anyway, most English houses are so draughty there's no need to seek fresh air – it comes to you.

I'm allergic to all forms of heartiness. I'm never happy in the company of rugger types, scrum of the earth with their plunge baths and sing-songs. When my husband played rugger regularly I loathed doing the teas – scraping fish paste on to margarine that had been scraped on to the bread by someone else. I wasn't wild about the wives either with their short hair and emerald-green trouser suits, bringing damp sponge cakes in tins they wanted back, and drinking halves of bitter in the club afterwards.

I also hate the way quite normal men get so hearty when they go sailing, putting on yachting caps, looking at you with far-seeing blue eyes, and yelling blue murder if you pull the wrong string.

My husband Leo went sailing only once. It was quite windy and every time someone shouted 'Leo' he said 'yes' and looked up, whereupon the boom would promptly swing round and knock him over. (It pays to know sailing terminology, if only as a protection.)

Of course the whole hearty sporting kick is basically anti-sex – cold baths, press-ups, deep breathing instead of heavy breathing, close your legs and open the windows. It seems a tragedy that all this excess energy should be exhausted on the rugger field or the gym, when it could be put to much more enjoyable use. As a favourite chum said: 'The best way of keeping fit is to have a Swedish mistress.'

But heartiness tends to be against any kind of personal relationship. Take the universal affability of MPs ra-raing and raising clasped hands above their heads. Take other professions who deal with large numbers of people: jolly bossy nurses, with the how-are-we-today approach, vicars and schoolmasters rubbing their hands and giving the impression of being marvellously interested in people. All these groups tend to use the hearty approach as a defence mechanism, to keep people at a distance, and avoid any kind of personal involvement.

Then there is the dreadful heartiness of television beer commercials, men in sports coats with froth on their lips, looking in at the local, and saying 'Yer know' every second sentence.

And of course heartiness is rampant on coach tours, or at holiday camps, or at those appalling Ladies' Nights, when red-faced men in paper hats take so much 'wain' with their own ladies during dinner they take liberties with everyone else's afterwards.

I shrivel when I have to join in Paul Jones, or the Hokey Kokey, or Knees up Mother Brown. My face stiffens with embarrassment during Auld Lang Syne or Happy Birthday to You-oo.

Finally, I detest heartiness in language: women who ask me how the 'babe' is, or refer to their lover as 'my chap', or their boss by his initials, and men who call their wives 'my bride'. Or awful talk about giving the 'youngsters' a chance, and describing people as 'lassies' or 'nice souls'.

But vomitoria of the decade came from an American hand-out which described me as a 'fine young British woman'. I have a sneaking feeling that I may die young of an acute hearty attack, and that in my obitchery they will write:

'This fine young British woman was an awfully good sort,' to which my games mistress would probably add, 'But now she's passed on, she's bound to be letting the Other Side down.' Heigh Ho, Chaps.

30 Do It Yourself

You can see them on Friday nights at Waterloo Station, terrorizing the crowds with their spray guns and their Black and Decker power drills, staggering under piles of hardboard, curtain rails, PVC tiling kits, paint pots and rolls of wallpaper.

It's the do-it-yourself brigade, hellbent for another weekend embellishing the home, knocking up cocktail cabinets in the loo, insulating the summer house or changing the wallpaper in the dog's kennel.

Or maybe they'll spend the weekend assembling that greenhouse they discovered last week on the mail-order page next to the corset ads.

My husband says the whole do-it-yourself movement is a desperate attempt to stave off boredom, If they weren't hitting nails, he claims, they'd be hitting their wives.

When we were engaged, I remember, I asked him how he intended to decorate the flat into which we were moving. He lay back on the sofa, and made what I thought then, with a thrill, was a deeply decadent remark: 'Gentlemen don't decorate,' he said. 'It is the business of the wealthy man to give employment to the artisan.'

So we were married – and for five years the paint peeled, the wallpaper curled, the dry rotted and the damp rose. Then we moved into our own house. Structurally it couldn't be faulted, but we couldn't take the décor: mauve pagodas, and bamboo with coy pandas downstairs; Robin and Batman, 007 and floral geometric upstairs; with the hall and landing an exhausted beige.

As we were broke, we came to the regretful conclusion that we'd have to decorate it ourselves.

In an attempt to get her house painted cheaply, a bossy friend held a painting party. Each guest was given a none-too-large drink and sent off with brush and paint – the greens to the spare room, the oranges to the larder, the cyclamens to the lavatory – and told to get on with it.

Through the evening my friend paced up and down like a foreman, ensuring that people really earned their next drink. Towards 11, however, the scarlets under the stairs mutinied, coinciding with the arrival of some drunks from another party. Chaos broke out and everyone started painting everything, including each other.

So we decided against a painting party and bought a book. 'The only way to do decorating,' said the first chapter, 'is properly.' How do you decorate improperly? we wondered. In the nude?

I compromised, and in bra and pants on the hottest day of the year started on the larder – approximately 3 ft. by 3 ft. Slap, slap, slapdash, went on the paint in great waves over the white ceiling . . . the window . . . and the floor. The colour that looked so subtle on the shade card, spread to vast deserts of ghastliness when it was on the wall. And it took me ten hours.

When he got home my husband tried to be tactful. 'The undercoat always looks frightful,' he said. 'It's the topcoat,' I said, and burst into tears.

Then there was the day we decided to paint the landing and the hall. I started downstairs painting indigo, my husband tackled upstairs with cranberry red. It never entered our heads that the colours would have to meet somewhere, and as he paints fast and badly, and I paint slowly and worse, we merged halfway up the stairs. The effect was curiously surrealistic.

We never realized the importance of dust sheets either. The carpet of each room now has a speckled border of paint. We were also extremely lazy, and whenever we came to a large wardrobe or desk against a wall we painted round it – so when we move, the Thames greens and the Prussian blues will be interspersed with large expanses of Batman and mauve pagodas.

Putting on wallpaper, however, was the worst. Our attempts to paper the spare room outcrazied even the Crazy Gang. We were so anxious not to undersoak the paper that it kept coming apart in our hands, and the bumpless tapioca pudding you put it on with got in our hair, on the floor, on the wrong side of the paper and all over the cats.

We lost our tempers and the scissors, we measured the pieces too short, we fell off the ladder and – although I'd bought enough paper to do the spare room and the adjoining passage (wildly expensive at eight guineas a roll) – we had to scrap so much we only managed to cover three-quarters of the bedroom.

We did the dining room last and were determined to do it properly. So for days we stripped away the pandas and the layers of floral nausea until we came to a layer of silver paper – and that came away, too, leaving a surface as pitted as the moon. We sanded and Polyfilled and, finally, on went the wallpaper: a glorious dragonfly blue. Alas, its glory only lasted a fortnight before it turned livid green and we realized that in our enthusiasm we'd stripped off the damp course.

So at last we called in the professionals, who did the room from top to toe, tiles on the floor, hessian on the walls. When the room was finished, its gleaming beauty prompted us to give a dinner party in its honour.

The weekend before, however, a post-honeymoon couple came to stay. They only appeared, yawning, for the occasional meals and their bedroom was immediately over the dining room. After they'd gone I was laying the table for the dinner party, when there was a noise like the Blitz, and down came the dining room ceiling – bringing all the hessian with it.

Staggering through the rubble, I telephoned the contractors round the corner. A little man in mauve trousers came mincing round in five minutes flat. 'No, dear, this won't do, will it,' he said, picking his way delicately over the debris. 'Why don't we knock all these walls through and go open plan?'

31 The Young Wife's Tale

You see her down the market in the lunch hour, battling through the crowds, scuttling from barrow to barrow to find the cheapest cauliflowers or peppers, weighed down by carrier bags and responsibilities.

Last month she was the dolly who blued her wages on clothes and make-up and took her washing home to Mother every week-end — now, in one stride, she is the newly married working wife who must be housekeeper, cook, hostess, laundress, seamstress, beguiling companion, glamour girl, assistant breadwinner and willing bedfellow rolled into one.

Looking back on the first fraught year of my marriage I realize we lived in total screaming chaos. I spent most of my time in tears — not tears of misery, but exhaustion. I couldn't cook, I couldn't sew, I had no idea about running a house, my knowledge of sex was limited to Eustace Chesser and Lady Chatterley — yet suddenly I was on trial: sexually, domestically, commercially, socially, and aware that I was inadequate on every count.

My husband's remarks like: 'Do you really think the book case is the right place for a mouldy apple?' would wound me to the quick — or that despairing 'Let's start as we mean to go on' as he looked at the flotsam of clothes strewn over the bedroom, and resented the fact that I had already appropriated five and three-quarters of the six drawers and three out of four of the coat hangers.

As we made love most of the night, I found it impossible to get up in the morning, cook breakfast, do my face and get out of the house by 8.15. Then followed an exhausting day at the office, only punctuated by one of those scurrying, shopping lunches. I was seldom home – due to the caprice of London Transport – before 7 o'clock. Then there was the bed to be made, breakfast to be washed up, the cat to be fed and chatted up, the day to be discussed and supper to be cooked. This was a proper supper (garlic, aubergines and all). The way to a man's heart was supposed to be through his stomach, so there was no getting away with pork pie or scrambled eggs. When I cooked Moussaka for the first time we didn't eat until one o'clock in the morning.

We were very gregarious and were asked out a great deal. My husband also played cricket and rugger at week-ends, so as a besotted newlywed I was only too happy to abandon the housework and watch him score tries and centuries.

As a result the flat became dirtier and more chaotic. The only time we ever really cleaned it up was when in-laws or relations came to stay, and my husband would then say that it was just like a barracks before the annual general inspection. 'How pretty those dead flowers look,' said a kindly aunt. 'Have they become fashionable in London?'

The only other possible moment to clean the flat was on my husband's occasional TA nights. Then I would hare round like a maniac, dusting and polishing; hoping, for once, to welcome him home scented and beautiful in a negligée with a faint smell of onions drifting from the kitchen. It never worked. Invariably he would let himself in unnoticed to find me tackling a mountain of dust under the bed with my bottom sticking out.

It was only after nine months, when the ice compartment wouldn't shut, that I learnt for the first time about defrosting the fridge. Things in the fridge were another headache. There were always those nine reproachful bowls of dripping, the tins of blackening tomato purée, the fish stock that never graduated into soup and the lettuce liquidizing in the vegetable compartment.

Laundry was another nightmare. It took me months to master the mysteries of the launderette. Very early on in our marriage, a red silk handkerchief found its way into the machine with the rest of the washing. My husband's seven shirts came out streaked crimson like the dawn, and for days he wore cyclamen underpants and claimed he was the only member of the fifteen with a rose-pink jock-strap. Once the washing was done it lay around in pillow cases for ages waiting to be ironed. My mother-in-law once slept peacefully and unknowingly on a pillow case full of wet clothes.

In fact my ironing was so disastrous that for a while we tried the laundry. This presented insuperable problems. One week we were too poor to get it out, the next week-end we'd be away, the next they'd shut by the time we got there, then finally we found they'd lost all our sheets. One laundry, we discovered afterwards from the butcher next door, was notorious for 'losing' sheets.

Our own dinner parties were not without incident. The first time my mother came to dinner the blanquette of veal was flavoured with Vim, and the chocolate mousse, left in the fridge all night, was impregnated with garlic and Kit-e-Kat. The cat once ate his way through two large packets of frozen scampi and, the night my husband's boss came to dinner, stripped the salad niçoise of its tunny fish and anchovies.

The flat, as I have said, got grimier and grimier, and the same week that a fungus began to grow under the sink I overheard someone say at a cocktail party that we lived in 'engaging squalor'. It was the last straw, and we hired a daily woman. It was not a success. I spent far more time than before cleaning up before she came, and after the first few weeks the standard went down. Then my husband came back one lunch hour and found her in our bed with the electric blanket and the wireless on.

The cats – we soon acquired a second – did not add to the ease of our married life. Whenever the doorbell rang I used to drench myself in scent to cover the smell of tomcat, and in summer there were fleas. The landlord forbade pets in the house, so the day he came to look over the flat the cats were locked in the wardrobe.

In spite of the 'engaging squalor', our spare room was permanently occupied; girls who had left their lovers or husbands who had left their wives, people who came from abroad or up from the country, all found a fleabitten home there. The hall was always full of carrier bags full of knickers or the cornucopian suitcases of birds of passage. One man came for two days and stayed for four months. One drunken Irishman who started rampaging lustfully round the flat in the still watches of the night was locked in his bedroom. Next morning we found him in the kitchen making coffee, and the imprint of his huge sleeping body remained outside on the long grass we called our lawn.

'When I was first married,' said a friend wistfully, 'I could never make mayonnaise. Humphrey kept kissing me and the oil would go in great dollops instead of drips, and the whole thing curdled. Now we've been married five years and can afford a mixer, and I make perfect mayonnaise every time now – it's my marriage that has curdled.'

We have been married seven years now – I still can't make mayonnaise – but we're not itching, and our marriage hasn't curdled. Even so I asked my husband to name, after seven years, the things that irritated him most about me.

His answers came out pat and immediate: using his razor on my legs and not washing it out; not putting tops back on tonic or soda water, or the ice tray back in the fridge; those little balls of Kleenex everywhere; the eighteen odd socks in his top drawer; the red rings of indelible lipstick on his handker-chief; running out of loo paper/soap/toothpaste; forgetting to turn off lights/fires/the oven; and, of course, my friends.

OK, OK, I said crossly. Then I remembered a poem by an American, which my husband had sent me when I was feeling suicidal early on in our marriage, which had suddenly made everything all right:

> My clumsiest dear, whose hands shipwreck vases,
> At whose quick touch all glasses chip and ring . . .
> Forgetting your coffee spreading on our flannel,
> Your lipstick grinning on our coat.
> So gaily in love's unbreakable heaven
> Our souls on glory of spilt Bourbon float.
> Be with me, darling, early or late, smash glasses,
> I will study wry music for your sake.
> For should your hands drop white and empty
> All the toys of the world would break.

32 Too Many Cooks and All That

Conversation became decidedly ribald the other evening when we had some people round for drinks, so I tactfully sent my thirteen-year-old stepdaughter out to get some ice. My protective instincts were misplaced, however, for when I went out to the kitchen a minute later to see if she were all right, she immediately asked me if I'd heard the following revised version:

> *Jack and Jill went up the hill*
> *To fetch a pail of water.*
> *Jill forgot to take the pill*
> *And now they have a daughter.*

This set me thinking that many of our proverbs and sayings could do with a bit of updating: *Better layed than never,* for instance, or *People in glass houses shouldn't throw orgies,* or on a more urgent contemporary theme: *Veni, Vici, VD.*

On the domestic front there's *The early bird who catches her hostess in the bath, Half a loaf is generally stale.*

And droppers in on Sunday night may have to choose between: *The devilled leftovers and the deep-freeze.*

Certainly *Too many cooks write cookery books.* My innate pessimism also claims that: *Inside every silver lining, there's a cloud trying to get out,* and who would deny that: *Early to bed, early to rise fouls up one's social life.*

And even though most proverbs rabbit on about the importance of friendship, *A friend in need is a bit of a nuisance.*

Then there are animals: *Empty pets make the most noise,* and

Bullies are not always cows, but what about the tragedy of the sausage factory forcing *Square pigs into round holes.*

There's plenty of advice for bachelors: *Over-familiarity breeds children.* Also *Big boys should be obscene and not heard* or *A bitch on time says 'why the hell are you late?'*

It's also a good idea if you're running more than two women to remember that: *Birds of a fella loathe each other.* And the greedy virgin is *Easier fed than done.*

A girl, on the other hand, shouldn't try to *Keep the wolf from the Dorchester* but must *Have more than one beau to her G-String.* At the same time remembering: *All's fair when you've had the roots touched up by the hairdresser.*

More topically, *No nudes is good news,* where Mrs Whitehouse is concerned, and the Women's Liberation Movement could easily use as their motto *A miss is as good as a male.*

Tourists perhaps might well remember that *When in Rome, you're invariably done by the Romans.*

Over the water, *Two blacks don't make a white* unless they want trouble.

There are even proverbs for the office: *A man is seldom known by the company he works for.* And: *All work and no play makes Jack the managing director,* and although we're sick of hearing it: *Many hands hate night work.*

Now drop-out country: *Go to the aunt, thou sluggard, she may be good for a fiver,* and *Never spoil the trip for a haporth of grass.*

Shot-gun weddings: *A bride comes after a fall.*

If you need a drink: *One swallow doesn't make you drunk,* and *In the kingdom of the blind-drunk, the pie-eyed man is king.*

Regrettably: *You can take a whore to the water, but she'd rather drink gin.*

Back at the ranch: *An Englishman's home is generally imperfectly heated* and *There's no place like home, it's far too untidy.*

When motoring: Always *Look before you leak,* you may be stung by nettles in the lay-by.

Which brings us back to the sex kick: *Spare the rod and spoil the masochist's fun,* or be like the sadistic, but amorous, schoolmaster who *Never canes but he paws.*

I suppose the motto of the stripper would be: *Grin and bare it.*

And you know, don't you, the moan of the ageing beauty:
Time, the great heel.

Finally as the queer trapeze artist said: '*Out of the flying pansy into the fairy.*'

33 A Nest of Gentlemen

What is a gentleman? Proverbially he prefers blondes and makes love on his elbows.

He doesn't pinch bottoms, or the bowling. He never serves underarm or in the Pioneer Corps. A gentleman never asks another man where he went to school, or interrupts him in the middle of a joke saying he's heard it before.

Writers throughout the ages have tried to define the term. 'A gentleman is one who never inflicts pain,' said Newman. Cowper suggested he was a man who never trod on worms. Byron believed a perfect gentleman never betrayed in his face what he was thinking – a good poker player, in fact. And who said a gentleman has such an innate respect for a man's lunch hour that he would never dream of asking anyone to come and see him before 3.30?

What of the non-gentleman? Peter Forster described him inspiredly as the kind of man who goes round pulling wings off country houses.

'May have been a perfectly good fellow,' was another interpretation from a cavalry officer, 'but he had buckles on his reins.'

The dictionary, however, defines the gentleman as 'A man of good birth, one who without a title bears a coat of arms, anyone over the rank of yeoman and the trading classes.'

Certainly, deep in his heart, every man thinks of himself as a gentleman, and also thinks that anyone above him or of a similar social standing is one, too. Anyone below, but with a good heart – an undergardener who likes children, for example – is known as 'one of nature's gentlemen'.

I don't think being a gentleman has anything to do with class. Ketas was not nearly as highly born as Shelley or Byron, but he was far more of a gentleman than either of them. Gentlemen know instinctively how to behave. They don't jump on girls without asking, or off buses without paying. They don't lick their fingers when turning pages, put buttons in the collection box, or use other people's telephones without offering to pay. A gentleman never corrects someone else's pronunciation. If his lunch date wants an advocado pear, let her have one.

Gentlemen don't read other people's letters, but they do read postcards. In other people's houses, they don't do the crossword or their hostess without asking. Gentlemen loathe maroon. I didn't think they ever winked either, until my father reminded me of a friend of his who said: 'When I see a pretty girl, I shut my eyes – one at a time.'

A gentleman's car and his clothes never look brand new. In fact the American humorist Shepherd Mead warns American girls to beware of the English gentleman because his suits are so well cut that you can never tell whether he's grossly over-weight or punily undersized until he's taken his clothes off – and by then it's too late. He also says the English gentleman has a corrugated bottom from being beaten so much at board-ing school.

Americans, on the other hand, even if their ancestors were sick all the way over on the *Mayflower*, are never really con-sidered true gentlemen by Englishmen.

Gentlemen, as a term, seems to me to spring from the seventeenth-century concept of chivalry, gifted amateurism, generosity of spirit, combined with a certain panache. Cavaliers were gentlemen, Roundheads were not. Hippies follow in the courteous Cavalier tradition, but definitely not skinheads.

Gentlemen inspire respect and love, rather than fear, and are therefore natural leaders. Bobby Moore is a gentleman. So are General Horrocks, Prince Charles, Derek Hart, Alistair Cooke and Jeremy Thorpe.

Gentlemen believe in doing their own thing, but it must be the decent thing. A gentleman would never dream of buying

112

wine by the half bottle, or getting in a stack of booze to beat the budget. If he offers you a drink in his house, he never goes into another room to pour it.

This gentlemanly disregard for matters financial is summed up by a young blood who complained to the police that his car had been stolen from the front of his club. Three days later, the police rang him up, and said they'd found the car – where he'd actually left it –behind the club. 'It's all right, thank you,' he said, 'I've got another one now.'

Blondes prefer gentlemen because their eyes don't swivel at parties, and they're just as polite to a beauty as to an old boot with carrier bags under her eyes.

A gentleman is also discreet – his wife never finds out he is erring and straying, nor does he carefully wait until she is past her prime and unlikely to get another man before he walks out on her.

Finally, no one can put a gentleman down better than another gentleman. I am reminded of the two soldiers who came into collision in a communication trench on a pitch-dark night.

'Who are you?' angrily asked one voice.

'And who may you be?' demanded the second.

'I am Major Sir Frank Swynnerton-Dyer, Coldstream Guards,' retorted the first.

'Oh, are you, indeed?' said the second. 'Well, I am Lieut. Col. Lord Henry Seymour, Grenadier Guards. I beat you on all three counts, get out of my way.'

34 On Being a Second Wife

I fell in love with my husband at a children's party when I was nine. A girl called Louise was rabbiting on about how many more acres her father had than anyone else's when my husband, then aged twelve, suddenly picked up a strawberry jelly and hurled it at her. His aim – as now – was true.

At school I wrote him rambling letters drenched in *Evening in Paris* ending 'I must stop now and go to choir practice'. At twenty-one he got married to someone else.

Six years later I met him by chance at a dinner party. His marriage had just broken up. He'd changed of course: tougher, more bitter, with a disconcerting habit of not laughing at my jokes, and of disagreeing with nine out of ten of my remarks. He referred constantly to his wife and the fact that she had left him.

I was extremely surprised when he asked me out the following night, and impressed and irritated that he didn't make a pass at me. On our second date we went to the theatre. Attempting to look sophisticated, I'd had my hair put up at vast expense. Much later that evening when he'd taken every pin out of my hair, he said I was never to put it up again as he'd decided he wanted to marry me. It seemed a good idea. There was just the question of his getting divorced from his wife.

At the time it didn't worry me that he'd been married before. It gave him glamour, mystery, an aura of tragedy. I would be the ministering angel that soothed away the pain and restored his faith in human nature. There were tremendous advantages too. Not only did he have experience but also furniture and kitchen utensils. Instead of pots and pans and toast racks, I could ask for pianos and Staffordshire dogs for wedding presents.

I hardly gave his first wife a thought. Anyone stupid enough to leave someone as lovely as him I felt wasn't worth considering. We had an idyllic summer playing hide and seek with the Queen's Proctor and taking my husband's daughter then aged five to the zoo on Saturdays. We were married in the autumn.

Trouble began soon afterwards, when he delivered his daughter back to his first wife one evening. He returned looking pale and unhappy. 'She was looking very pretty,' he admitted later. 'She gave me that special sideways look under her eyelashes and I wanted her like hell.'

Although I was knocked for six, I don't think I made an issue of it at the time.

A few weeks later she rang up. I answered the telephone. In a husky, I thought consciously sexy voice she asked if she might speak to my husband. They gossiped for three-quarters of an hour, by which time I had been reduced to tears.

I began to worry that he never said anything derogatory about her. 'At least it means if you leave him he won't bitch about you,' said a friend, which didn't help much.

Little by little, this first wife was becoming an obsession. Suddenly her possessions seemed to litter the flat, sheets with her name tapes on, books with her name written inside – they all appeared to be Bibles or prayer books – address books of people they had both known, anthologies with love poems underlined, old dress patterns, scent bottles, odd shoes.

Whenever my husband went out, I ransacked his desk, lacerating myself reading old love letters she had written him, or letters he had written her and never posted.

Jealousy gnawed at me for those years they'd spent together. Had he only married me to staunch the wound, because he needed a housekeeper, a hostess at his table, because I adored him and because he fancied me? My obsession was driving me into prolonged black moods. I kept making plans to wait in a café outside her flat in North London so, unbeknown to her, I could see what she was really like.

My husband decided it might help if I met her. So, on Christmas Eve, we called in for a cup of coffee. Determined to appear at though I did this sort of thing every day, I'd spent all afternoon putting on my makeup to look as though I wasn't wearing any.

She, by contrast, looked like the Queen of the Night – black sweater, black leather skirt, fishnet stockings, jet earrings, black nail polish and lashings of black eye make-up. We sat round being excessively polite, studying each other when we thought the other wasn't looking. I'd never reckoned she'd be that attractive. She seemed to thrum with sex.

We had a merry Christmas after that with me in tears most of the time. I knew I was being selfish, and it didn't help realizing that my misery was motivated more by furious jealousy than by worry that he might still be in love with her.

Was she better in bed than me? I kept asking my husband. She was different, he replied tactfully.

Another distressing factor was that I didn't have children, and in five years while I ricocheted from one specialist to another, she remarried and went on to produce four more children.

The first two years I was married were the worst. Our fourth wedding anniversary was a landmark – it meant I had been married to my husband longer than she had.

Then she went to America and later we heard she was separating from her second husband to marry a third. At least I was better at staying married than she was.

Ironically, what really laid the ghost was my falling in love three years ago with another man who fell in love with me to such an extent that it rocked my marriage to its foundations. After appalling unhappiness on all sides, the whole thing blew over, having taught me what I wanted to know all the time – that my husband really loved me, needed me and would have been devastated if I'd left him.

It also made me realize that my husband's first wife was not a man-eater, nor a monster of depravity, but merely a woman who had fallen in love with someone else while she was married.

Last October we adopted a baby. It has been an unqualified success, and has put the final nail in the coffin of my obsession.

116

35 A Child's View of Heaven

It saddens me that I have no religion. I was an intensely devout little girl. Every morning I rushed to the mirror hoping I'd sprung a halo overnight like the Cookeen ads. Every night I spent hours praying for every individual cat, dog, pony and hen that I knew. I even enjoyed church and complained bitterly when I was taken out before the sermon.

I thought continually about my Guardian Angel. What sex was he? How was he constructed? In the end I decided he was sexless and went straight round underneath like a Teddy bear.

Religion walked in the family of course. My grandfather was a canon and I always pestered my mother for anecdotes of vicarage life when she was a child; how the bishop buttered his table mat instead of his bread when he came to lunch, how a bucket of water intended for a stray dog drenched the curate, how my aunt secretly added the cat's and dog's names to my grandmother's prayer list, so the entire Mother's Union were exhorted to pray for the return to health of Mewkins and Raggety Bones.

I think I began to go off religion when I went to kindergarten. I played the Ass in a nativity play and had to sing a song about:

Standing knee high in the straw,
Makes me love the baby more.

I was supposed to make my entrance after the Ox had mooed his bit. Unfortunately I caught sight of my mother in the audience, shrieked with joy, and completely missed my cue. Afterwards I was sharply reprimanded by the head mistress. 'You spoilt our play,' chorused the other little girls.

It's like the one about a small boy who started off playing Joseph and was demoted to the Innkeeper because he was so naughty. All went well on the day until Mary and Joseph rolled up at the Inn and asked if there were any room: 'Masses of room for everyone,' said the Innkeeper blandly. 'Come in at once.'

I might have retained a remnant of faith if religion hadn't been so rammed down my gullet at boarding school. Not only did we have to go to services twice a day, and three times on Sunday, but it was also extremely high church. Brought up on matins, I was appalled by the incense, the bells, the genuflecting and crossing, the weedy acolytes dressed in laundry bags, the sing-song chant of the priest, and what seemed to me endless tippling of wine. I caused a furore by refusing to kneel down in Creed. But, threatened with expulsion, I naturally capitulated. I was not the stuff of martyrs.

Later I took my revenge. We had a large imposing house mistress called Miss Body. One evening I and three cronies, draped in sheets, with dressing-gown cords round our waists, staged a protest march through the dormitories. The leader bore a cross made of precariously roped-together rulers. She was followed by two acolytes swinging Morny's French Fern in place of censers. I brought up the rear (pillows tied under my sheet to resemble the vicar's paunch).

'This is Miss Body, who is given for thee,' I chanted.

'It is meet and right so to do,' sang the others, stuffing handkerchiefs into their mouths to muffle their giggles.

We were just beginning to swing when we rounded the corner, slap into the house mistress herself. Great was her wrath. She couldn't expel all four of us, however, as it would have deprived the school of an income of £1,400 a year. Instead all treats were suspended to the end of term.

The fight went out of me after that. I dispelled the tedium of those everlasting sermons by exploring the prayer book, learning about the churching of women, and the numerous kith I couldn't marry, like my husband's sister's son, and reading the prayers for famine and dearth (we never thought we got enough to eat at school).

Ironically though, it was at my confirmation that I finally

parted company with religion. The build-up was so fantastic: a whole year of intensive instructions, hours of meditation alone in one's cubicle, flowers, hundreds of confirmation cards, the nunlike fervour of the other candidates.

I was going through a spotty stage at the time. And in preceding weeks, I bargained endlessly with God: 'Make me spotless of face on the day, and I promise to be spotless of sin.'

Confirmation day dawned, I had more spots than ever. Dressed in a white dress and veil of disfiguring ugliness, like something someone's Nanny left out in the rain, I stumped up the aisle to receive the bishop's sign – a vision of angels, a still small voice. Nothing happened – not the flicker of a flaming sword. Anti-climax was inevitable. I never took religion seriously again. The only thing that bothered me next morning, when I took my first communion, was composing my face in a suitably pious expression when I walked back to my seat.

Recently I was faced with the problem of whether to try and bring up our child religiously. We had our son christened as a matter of course. The service was full of incident. He wore the family christening robes, and, deeply resentful of being in drag, bellowed with rage throughout the service. We had difficulty in keeping straight faces when the vicar walked in with a steaming electric kettle and emptied it into the font. Worse was to come – when the vicar took the baby from one of his very pretty godmothers, he gathered up her skirt with the folds of the christening robes, and her scarlet knickers were displayed to the startled congregation.

I was also appalled by the toughness of the promises the godparents had to make for my son. I'm not sure I want him to renounce the vain pomp and glory of the world and the carnal desires of the flesh before he's had time to sow even one tiny wild oat. And how can a baby be expected to fight manfully against the Devil under Christ's banner?

And education is such a headache. The other day I heard the story about a man who arrives at the Gates of Heaven and is staggered to be welcomed by the Devil.

'What on earth are you doing here?' he asks.

'Oh,' replies the Devil. 'We've gone comprehensive.'

36 *No News Is Good News*

The world is much too much with us. Late and soon, disaster, famine, wars and strife are thrust down our throats. Day and night, we are assaulted with hourly news bulletins, newspaper reports and hour upon impossibly boring hour of current-affairs programmes on television.

I have a complete block about current affairs. I don't want to know what's going on in the world. We always fight on Monday night because my husband wants Panorama and I crave the lush escapism of Man at the Top, and much as I love Messrs Bosanquet and Dimbleby, I always go and read in the bath during News at Ten and Twenty-Four Hours.

I get so fed up with seeing heads of state arriving at No. 10 for Ted and breakfast, and hearing the television pundits going round and round in informed circles. I'm bored stupid by outside broadcasters, standing in the long grass or on piles of wreckage, looking urgent in their shirt sleeves and crackle-crackling on about the Muddle East and Palestinian gorillas.

I'm mystified too by what's happening in Ireland and the Far East. And African politics are quite beyond me – and them too it seems. If only everyone stayed in power a bit longer. I had only got used to Obote when he was supplanted by General I Amin, and who is to say he won't be General I Am Out by the end of the week?

The names are the big problem in current affairs. How can anyone take seriously someone called U Thant (except Nancy Mitford) or Jarring, or Wasfi Tel or Yassir Arafat – he sounds like a new brand of margarine. Why can't they have nice simple double-barrelled names like our politicians?

I find it rather shaming the way one remembers more about the sexy ones: Mayor Lindsay, Mr Gorton and General Dayan, or that self-styled Playboy of the Western World, Prime Minister Trudeau. I would find it much easier to work up an interest in the TUC if they looked more glamorous and abandoned their hair cream and short back and fronts – although walrus moustaches make a change.

I'm as bad with newspapers as television. I skip the long responsible pieces on the social services and the mark hitting the dollar ceiling, and swoop on trivia about Princess Anne's moodiness or Mr Obote's underpants.

I sometimes wonder what foreigners think when they read about the activities in the House of Commons with their pairings and whips and Black Rod. No wonder we have this reputation for the *Vice Anglais*, and barbarism too when you get headlines about: 'Guillotine cuts off Mrs Castle in midsentence.'

I am afraid I have much in common with my favourite teenage cousin who has an 8 ft. placard absolutely weighed down with coats of emulsion from different demonstrations. Unfortunately he's always getting the demo wrong, and arriving down at the Dilly after concussing several people in the Tube, to find he's painted 'Hands off Bernadette' when it's 'Hands off Rudi' week.

He and I, however, are not alone in our political ignorance. Take that mammoth yawn the Common Market. To the average Englishman, there's nothing like a Dane except a Swede or a Norwegian, and the only thing he knows about Luxembourg is that Pete Murray was born there on 208 metres twenty years ago.

That's why he can't work up much enthusiasm about Britain's proposed entry. Certainly few subjects have been more flogged to death, you can't turn on the box without some troll from the Black Forest droning on about the political implications or the price of butter. What intrigues me is that no one so far has considered the sexual aspect.

Will our native shores suddenly be flooded with thousands

of French commercial travellers peddling their wares, putting their basketweave toes in the door and being sharply told: 'Pas aujourdhui, merci.'

Will German companies based over here be inundated with irate telephone calls from English husbands telling them to 'Keep your Hans off my wife'. And how will the bowler-hatted English trader fare abroad? I hope that once he's crossed the Channel, he remembers to sleep on the right side of the bed.

In all that desperate palaver about decimal coinage and distances, you'd think someone would have considered the literary implications. It may be very well for Geoff the Ripon to woo M. Pompidou with the cry of 'I'd run a million kilometres for one of your smiles', but it will reduce the Old Vic to a state of uproar if Shylock starts clamouring for his 0·453 kilo of flesh.

I find the whole concept of the shrinking world terribly depressing. Still, one must move with the times, and in a few years no doubt I shall be putting on my flying helmet and goggles and telling my husband: 'Just popping down to the Global Village to do some shopping, darling.'

37 *Frustration Is...*

Frustration is opening an unsealed enveloped and finding a change of address card instead of a party invitation, or arriving at a party just as the most beautiful man you've ever seen in your life is leaving.

Frustration is tottering to the bathroom, groaning with a hangover, and discovering that the only remaining Alka Seltzer which was going to save you from death until the shops open is that horrible bit of pith they put in the top.

Frustration is a burst hot-water bottle, or the bottom of a carrier bag full of groceries collapsing just as you're running for a bus, or the Hoover pegging out half an hour before your mother-in-law comes to stay.

Frustration is seeing someone you love from the top of a bus, or the transistor battery running out in the middle of a Mozart piano concerto, or being unable to translate foreign quotations in a book.

Frustration is putting on a new pair of tights and finding the crutch only comes up to knee level, or leaving your cheque book behind, or forgetting to put that half-crown into the launderette.

Frustration is loathing every moment of a holiday you're paying a fortune for; or waking up just as unmentionably delicious things are about to be done to you in a dream; or insomnia when you've decided to get your first early night in weeks.

Frustration is trying to get into last year's dresses, or to get that plastic hairbrush back into its handle, or spilling make-up over a white dress just as you're about to go out.

Frustration is using the wrong side of the Sellotape, or having a bottle of gin but no tonic, or the local bore getting into the same carriage just as you've started *Portnoy's Complaint*.

Frustration is losing the tin-opener when seven ravenous cats are mewing round your feet, or being about to tell a brilliantly apposite story at a dinner party, when some idiot changes the subject.

Frustration is droppers-in when you've just gone up to bed for the afternoon, or the telephone ringing just as you've got into a hot bath, or staying in to watch a film on television that you missed the last seven times around, when a chum turns up with a suitcase saying she's left her husband.

Frustration is buying a dress in a sale, and going round the corner where a sale isn't on and finding the same dress for half the price.

Frustration is other people talking about people you don't know, or a friend saying: 'Samantha's just told me a stunning bit of gossip, but she made me swear not to tell you.'

Frustration is running out of flour when you're about to make a white sauce before a dinner party or knowing your hairdresser has three long-haired customers to comb out before you, and your lunch hour was up half an hour ago.

Frustration is routing out your bikini, plastering yourself with Ambre Solaire, finding sunglasses and all the letters you've been meaning to answer for six months, stretching out on the rug – and then the sun goes in.

Frustration is getting down to a really scurrilous lunch with a workmate when you feel a heavy hand on your shoulder and the personnel officer says: 'May I join you?'

Frustration is train strikes, and Oxford Street Tube station at 5.30 p.m., and buses that deliberately go slow, and some lusty youth nipping in to your seat when you've just stood up to give it to some doddering old lady.

Frustration is losing one shoe, or forgetting what you were going to say, or locking yourself out, or searching frantically for your bus fare and joyfully discovering a lead weight in the lining of your husband's coat which you think is a shilling.

Frustration is getting a letter which fails to enclose a cheque, or lovers sitting in front of you at the cinema – particularly when they're both wearing spectacles and sound like the clashing of antlers.

Frustration is people parking in front of your garage, or a stranger reading a riveting letter in front of you on the bus and turning over before you get to the bottom of the page.

Frustration is not having someone to tell when something marvellous happens, frustration is not having someone, frustration is a ravishing queer, or that used sachet of shampoo that won't go down the loo.

Frustration is trying to think of punchlines to end articles.

38 Black and White

There's never a dull moment in SW6. Last Thursday I was involved in a racial incident. The morning started badly anyway. Six people were coming to dinner, the baby was teething and had been crying all morning, a gang of roadmen were having fun with a pneumatic drill outside, and I had a mountain of work to finish.

At twelve o'clock, however, the baby went to sleep and the roadmen to lunch, so I sat down at my typewriter. The next moment the doorbell rang. I was expecting the electrician so I answered it. There was nobody there. I returned to work. The doorbell rang again – still nobody there. But I could hear muffled giggling; it was the children in the street playing at ringing and running away. I told them in no uncertain terms to get lost, and went back to my work.

They went on ringing my bell and running away for the next two hours, whereupon the baby woke up and started yelling. The doorbell rang yet again. It was the last straw. I went upstairs, filled a bucket with water and emptied it at random into the street. Blow me, if I didn't drench the only black child involved and miss all the white children.

Within thirty seconds the black child's parents, who both stand 6 ft. 3 in. in their stockinged feet, were screaming abuse at me. Not only would they report me to the police, but the NSPCC and the Race Relations Board. Their child hadn't rung the bell, they claimed, why had I picked on him? Because he was the only black one?

If I had been a man, said the husband advancing, he'd have beaten me up. The wife, thrusting herself forward with

clenched fist, seemed to have no such scruples. Finally, muttering dire threats they went back to their house.

I spent a miserable afternoon and in the end went out and
bought the biggest box of chocolates I could find, and
knocked on the black couple's door. The flood victim
appeared, his face spread into a grin and he yelled for his
mother. She appeared looking surly, but cheered up when I
apologized profusely, and said we couldn't afford to have
rancour between us in the same street. Eventually she
managed a half smile and accepted the chocolates.

Since the incident, the child has been tricycling up and
down looking longingly at our window. A quick dousing, I
suppose, is nothing compared with a large box of chocolates.
In this recent cold spell, he has been wearing shorts and the
thinnest cotton tee-shirt, so he's bound to get pneumonia,
and I expect I shall be blamed for that as well.

The most depressing aspect of the incident has been the
reaction of the rest of the street. Since Thursday, every white
has rushed to congratulate me: 'Glad you got tough with them
blacks, high time someone taught them a lesson.'

When I protested they'd got it wrong, they merely shook
their heads knowingly, saying they were on my side and there
was no need to explain. Equally the black people living in the
street, with whom hitherto I have passed the time of day most
amicably, now sidle past with downcast eyes.

I wonder if anyone, like me, finds the whole race question
extremely irritating. I have a number of black friends, and
they are friends not because or in spite of their colour, but
because they are amusing, intelligent and I hope fond of me.
In the same way, I have friends who are Chinese, French,
German, American, what you will. They are all people who
don't bore me, and the day someone can turn to a black man,
and say in all honesty: 'As a person, I find you a godawful
bore,' and the black man won't take it racially, we shall have
taken a major step forward to solve the race problem.

People are so extreme about race, like the whites in our
area, who haven't a good word for the blacks and see them as a
constant threat to their jobs and homes.

On the other hand, I'm not sure my kind of hypocrisy isn't

127

worse. If a white man tries to pick me up in the street, I tell him to go jump in the lake, but if it's a black man, I spend at least a quarter of an hour explaining that I'm married with a baby, so his feelings aren't hurt.

It's the same at parties. People always crowd round a black man, even if he is a bore, merely to be seen doing the right thing. Anyone who wants a good laugh should go to a Hampstead Left-wing intellectual party, and watch the anguished faces of those middle-aged wives so terrified of displaying prejudice that they let agile young Africans take every liberty with them on the dance floor. Oh, it's great to be black in NW3!

It's a pity we can't see other people with the uncorrupted vision of children. The first time my five-year-old niece saw a black man was when she and my sister-in-law sat in front of one on the top deck of a bus: To my sister-in-law's intense embarrassment, the child kept craning round to look at him.

'Mummy,' she said eventually, 'do look at that man.' My sister-in-law, acutely aware that the rest of the bus was listening, told her somewhat briskly to shut up. But my niece was not to be daunted: 'Just look at that man,' she went on, 'he's got a moustache just like Grandaddy.'

I wish blacks and whites would learn to treat each other as human beings – to be liked, loved or disliked, but not because of the colour of their skin. Our cat, emulating the young lady of Starkie, has just had her kittens, two white, two black and one Khaki. All the kittens will be loved irrespective of colour, but the one with the nicest nature will be loved the most.

39 A Mobile Seducer's Guide

'Can a chap be a Romeo in an Alfa Romeo ?' said a High Court judge recently. To try and find the ideal car for would-be seducers I set out to do a bed test on nine of the latest models.

'Of course the biggest crumpet-catcher of them all,' said the man at the Chequered Flag, 'is the Shelby Mustang, Steve McQueen's car in *Bullitt*.'

We were sitting, or rather lying, in a buttercup-yellow Lotus Europa. The position was frankly erotic, but we were so completely divided from each other by the massive transmission tunnel that it was like being in single beds. In fact, despite its sexy external appearance, the Lotus is so small inside that it is guaranteed to defeat the most enterprising sexual athlete. There is no mirror for the girl to detousle herself afterwards.

Bonus point: the Lotus is ideal for voyeurs. Mini-skirted girls have to bend double to get in and out.

How about a Cadillac, I thought? Smooth, dignified, with all the plushy appeal of American big business, the Eldorado Convertible is the car for sugar daddies. There is no transmission tunnel in front, so the driver can while away traffic jams playing gentle footy-footy. Press a button and the windows shut, press another and the doors lock, so unless a girl knows her way round a Cadillac she can't escape. No gear levers or handbrake divide the driver from his quarry and the front bench seat makes for easy pouncing. Bonus points for middle-age spreaders are the tilt and telescopic steering and, remembering a cold woman is a cold woman, the driver can always resort to the air-conditioning to whip the temperature up to a torrid 84 degrees in seconds.

But although the front seat would accommodate two horizontal dwarfs there is not really room enough in the car for comfortable seducing. Much better take to the woods or to the Dorchester.

Urbane, sleek as an otter, the Rover 2000 was voted by *Drive* Magazine the car that women would most like the man in their life to own. One of the reasons was probably because the seduction possibilities of the 2000 are negligible. There's not enough room in the back, and although the front seats recline fully the driver is separated from his passenger by a hefty transmission tunnel and a potentially emasculating handbrake.

According to the brochure, 'the steering wheel is adjustable for rake': libertines please note. For heavy travellers there's an enormous boot; for heavy breathers there's an optional heated rear window. It is described, understandably, as the 'safest car on the road'.

Next, the E-Type, deliberately built in the shape of a phallic symbol. This is *the* girl puller, the car that cricks necks in the High Street. But, like the Lotus Europa, it is almost impossible to seduce anyone inside. Passengers and drivers again sit separated, by a transmission tunnel as big as the Berlin Wall, and the only advance the driver can really make is to lean over and tickle his passenger's ankle when he lets her out – the locks are set very low in the car.

For the enterprising, on the other hand, there's always the bonnet, or a large boot which can be enlarged by putting the back seat forward to take two, if they don't mind their feet sticking out in the open. Not for people with chilblains. No mirror provided, and if the girl gets scared watch out she doesn't press the Hazard Warning button, and set all four indicators flashing for help.

Bonus point: with a maximum speed of 160 m.p.h., this is the car that will whip her back to your flat fastest.

The Ford Executive is 'not so much a car, more a spacious lounge', according to the brochure, which goes on to rhapsodize about 'wall to wall carpeting', and the 'magnificent upholstery in genuine crushed hide' (the car's is not the only hide that's going to be crushed if the seducer has his way). A wireless and two speakers are thrown in, but you have to provide your own flying ducks.

The front seats recline very comfortably, divided only by a flat console, and even the door handles are padded, so if the girl goes temporarily berserk with passion she won't hurt herself. There is a sun roof through which she can escape if necessary.

Radford's have converted the Mini Cooper into a Mini Rolls, with a £3,000 price tag. The car certainly looks sensational. Seats recline, there's a spotlight, a sunroof, an estate-car door at the back, electric windows, a wireless, a tape recorder with two speakers, a cigarette lighter, and numerous other refinements including an 'ergonomically laid-out fascia'.

But from a seducer's viewpoint the car is no great shakes. The seats are too small, too far apart, and there's no room for any enthusiastic gambolling in the back, although the back seat folds forward to enlarge the boot. Very impressive, but too brisk, business-like and contrived to be really seductive as a car. It lacks the casual charm of the Lotus or the E-Type.

The little Fiat, on the other hand, is visually a car with tremendous panache and charm. The bonnet resembles a sexy Italian thrusting out his chest. Inside, however, though the front seats adjust fully, they are again too far apart and divided by the gear lever. In the back there's room for only two if they don't breathe out.

From a seducer's point of view, this is yet another car for contortionists. The only possible way to make love seems to be standing up with the sunroof open, as though you were in an armoured car. Ideal for former Desert Rats. The back seat pushes forward to provide a substantial boot. Excellent for easy parking if you don't like being stood up.

The Rolls-Royce Phantom VI, however, is the real passion wagon, a true transport of love. There's enough room in the back to have a love-in cocktail party. And to put you in the mood they've provided a cocktail cabinet complete with four glasses, two decanters and a bottle-opener. In the arm-rest on the back seat you'll find a cigarette case, note-book for jotting down telephone numbers, and two mirrors so you can ensure your hair is brushed carefully over the bald patch. Press-buttons turn off lights, close windows, and shut off the chauffeur with a glass panel.

Or if your girl friend has a Lady Chatterley complex, you can always buy a peaked hat, sunglasses and a bottle of lager and sit in the front with her. Its cavernous boot would accommodate a year's luggage or even a wheelchair.

Finally, the Volkswagen Variant 1600, an estate car which, of all the nine models, seems the car in which the wolf is most likely to succeed. As the brochure points out: 'An increasing number of bachelors have discovered you don't need three children to have a Variant.' On the other hand, if you get a Variant you may suddenly find you've got three children, if you're not careful.

For, as the brochure continues, 'the bachelors can pack in boats, camping clobber, and if they put down the back seat they will have even more room to play with': yes indeed, about 25 sq. ft. – enough to accommodate the most elongated couple. Here at last is the *lebensraum* seducers have been searching for.

The Variant's front seats recline to forty-nine positions, which is a good start, and even the doors are provided with safety locks, and 'won't fly open however hard the impact'. The ideal car for seducers, in fact.

40 *On Sexy Men*

What makes a man sexy? Fancying me, for a start. I'm not attracted to men unless I think they're attracted to me. And they must know how to use their eyes. It's those hard, lingering stares that start the electricity crackling.

Flattery is vital too (convince a woman she's got a marvellous body, and she'll be far more inclined to let you see more of it). But it must be subtle – not like the gibbermaking man who came up to me at a party the other day.

'Forgive my interferring with you,' he purred. 'But you are most beautiful woman I haf ever seen.' His name was Seraphim and he was Cuban and we were just tuning in to each other's vibrations when some married friends came over.

'May we come and talk to you,' said the husband. 'I don't know about you,' said Seraphim playfully, 'but your wife, of course. She is most beautiful woman I haf ever seen.' Well, I lost interest after that. I don't care for men who hedge their bets.

I don't like mean men either – like the awful wallet fumbler who tries to fob you off with half a bottle of the sort of wine you have to take your knife and fork to, on the pretext that he adored it in Cyprus last year.

Although I am unashamedly attracted to successful men, I don't like men who boast of their sexual conquests. Nor men who list their failures. If his wife and ten previous girl friends didn't understand him, what's in it for me? And I find myself losing interest in men who flash their teeth at themselves every time they pass a looking glass or who put Saccharine in their coffee.

Being a hot-blooded nine and a half stone, I prefer big broad-shouldered men to mini-boys. But a huge, pink-faced handsome Englishman often leaves me cold, while a skinny little boy with bedroom eyes reduces me to instant turmoil.

Appearances, in fact, are hard to generalize about, although one friend asserts: 'Halitosis, dirty finger nails, and four mentions of Mummy on the trot is a four-star non-lay.'

I like men who bath often and wear masses of scent. I'm allergic to sandals, particularly worn with socks, white polo-neck sweaters, woolly hats with pom-poms, pipes and men who hide their baldness under Rex Harrison hats. I hate backs of necks, so a man's hair must curl over his collar – but it mustn't protrude from his nostrils, or sprout in tufts from his cheekbones. Built-up shoes, canary-yellow V-necks worn next to the skin, black lacy see-through tops, matching ties and handkerchiefs, anoraks and Day-glow bow-ties are also out.

I hate hippy clothes on older men, but trousers must look as though they're glued to the body over the hips and thighs. Cigars, cigarette-holders, fur coats and dark glasses are all sexy. So is not going to sleep for three days. Men always look good with bags under their eyes.

Decadent men, in fact, I find irresistible, but in the early stages I prefer them to behave like the gentlemen they aren't. I also have a weakness for men who grow old disgracefully.

At a dinner-party, the other night, I sat next to a distinguished octogenarian. Our hostess was on his other side. Before we had even tucked into the caviar, I felt his heavy hand on my leg, and pressure continued throughout the meal. I also noticed he bolted his food. Afterwards my hostess told me: 'I say, Sir Timothy had his hand on my thigh all the way through dinner.' No wonder he ate so fast.

I also like men to be discreet, and not charge round London on roller-skates with a megaphone, telling all. Nor was I amused when a man who failed to make me turned the tables by sending a bunch of roses to my office saying 'God, you were great, darling' on a note read by the entire typing pool.

The hard-to-get type I find fascinating. When I was eighteen I fell in love with a boy in the office and asked him to dinner one Monday. He couldn't, he was going out with his mother. Tuesday? He was taking granny to the dogs. Wednesday? He had to play squash. Thursday? He thought frantically for a moment. 'No,' he said. 'Thursday's no good. It's my day for doing things.'

But is there an ideal man? The conventional glamour boys – Steve McQueen, Omar Sharif, Scott Walter, James Fox, Danny la Rue – leave me pretty unmoved. I think Cy Grant, the singer, is the best-looking man I've seen. I love Michael Caine, and for sheer sex appeal Robert Mitchum takes a lot of beating.

But on the whole I prefer the more cerebral type: the late Adlai Stevenson, Lord Harlech, Giulini, Giscard D'Estaing, the French Finance Minister, the devastating Michael Charlton of Panorama, and the gentle, great-hearted, unpredictable, Rabelaisian Leo Cooper – my husband.

Bw 71